From French Fries to a Franchise:
A Macca's Memoir

From French Fries to a Franchise

A Macca's Memoir

MICHELE LAYET

Copyright © Michele Layet 2018

All rights reserved. No part of this publication may be reproduced, stored in a retrieval system or transmitted in any form by any means, electronic, mechanical, photocopying, recording or otherwise, without the prior written permission of the publisher and copyright holder. Michele Layet asserts the moral right to be identified as the author of this work.

Published by Michele Layet

Typeset by BookPOD

Front cover inspired by an original artwork from Hugh Evans

Back cover photo Charlie Bell and Michele Layet

ISBN: 978-0-646-99151-1 (pbk)
eISBN: 978-1-925457-86-5 (e-book)

For Joan and Robert Layet
My exceptional parents

In memory of
Charlie Bell and Graham Goldenberg

Contents

1. Would You Like Fries With That?........................1
2. Silence is Golden 7
3. The Highway to Cheltenham 15
4. The True Meaning of PC.................................21
5. Would You Like a Stat With That?................27
6. The Dress Rehearsal..35
7. Showtime 43
8. The Encore..51
9. McChelt Chatter 59
10. Hamburger University....................................65
11. Orange Bowl Shenanigans 77
12. Ronald McDonald Was Not the Only Clown................81
13. Fundraising and McLaLa Day 89
14. The Board, the Watch and the Ten Year Ring................95
15. My Own Golden Arches 99
16. The Grand Opening 113
17. Now Hiring 117
18. Would You Like a Smile with That?............ 123
19. Many Happy Returns 137
20. Flag Protocol 147
21. Crew Uniforms... 151
22. Co-operatively Speaking............................... 155
23. Is This A Paid Position? 163
24. Be Daring, First and Different 169
25. Simply About Charlie 175
26. Hooroo, Now I'm A Macaroo 179
27. The Car Park 185
    Acknowledgements 189

Chapter 1

Would You Like Fries With That?

'Here's your uniform,' said my manager as he handed me a pile of folded clothes.

'Thanks, but, er ... this looks like a man's shirt ...'

'There aren't any female managers.'

'Right ...'

When I began work at the McDonald's South Oakleigh store in April 1982, there were no female manager's uniforms, no breakfast menu and no Happy Meals. Drive-thru restaurants were new and 30 cent cones hadn't yet been invented. It was just over ten years since the first Australian McDonald's restaurant had opened in Sydney in December 1971.

I commenced my management training program at South Oakleigh and during orientation the store manager gave me a tour, a couple of pale yellow men's shirts and some petty cash to buy two beige skirts of my choice. I declined the offer of a tie; at that time men's ties were so wide you could almost land a plane on them. It was a time of perms, shoulder pads, corduroy pants and desert boots.

Michele Layet

In 1982 I was armed with an arts degree, some smarts, and the ego of a 23-year-old with a European gap year behind me. Actually, gap years didn't exist then; school leavers just took off while deciding what to do next.

My university major was in environmental science (fluvial geography, to be exact) but to my dismay I discovered I was underqualified for the jobs I applied for. Deflated after six months of interviews and knockbacks, I answered an ad in *The Age* newspaper for a trainee management position—no experience required. As I had none I was perfect for the job. My interview with Head Office Regional Manager Don Kissel went well and soon after I received an offer of consideration from McDonald's Australia. But—there is always a but—first I had to attend a three day on-the-job evaluation to determine my compatibility with the company.

That first trial day on the job coincided with the first time in McDonald's Australia history that stores traded on Good Friday. Putting me to the test, the duty manager rostered me to work on Fries and Filet-O-Fish. An American owner-operator in the US invented the Filet-O-Fish—with a store in a predominantly Catholic area, he needed a new burger to counteract declining sales on Friday nights during Lent. But I digress. Never in my life had I worked so hard. I thought I knew all about hard work; in earlier jobs I'd collected lost golf balls at the Box Hill golf course, worked every weekend at an old people's home for three years and over University summer breaks, packed chicken pieces at Golden Poultry in Somerville for KFC.

I survived the three-day trial but went home and told Mum

From French Fries to a Franchise

I'd been so slow I didn't expect to get the job. Instead, I was hired and so began 26 years in the only full-time job I ever had.

On my first day as an employee I was introduced to my trainer, Irene. She became my go-to guru for all things McDonald's. She knew her customers by name and held the title 'Crew Trainer', while my badge read 'Trainee Manager'. Usually McDonald's managers and senior staff came from within the crew ranks, having worked their way up the corporate ladder. But not me. I had to be trained in all the basics: store procedures, maintenance, front counter, grill, buns, dress, chicken, dining room, deliveries, stock-count, ordering, rostering and managing staff.

At McDonald's each individual is trained thoroughly in one task at a time. My first training station was Thick Shakes. Irene explained that in the 1950s Ray Kroc, the American founder of McDonald's, had bought the marketing rights to a five-spindle multi-mixer to increase his paper-cup sales. His biggest customers were Walgreen Drugs (the largest drug store chain in the US) and Dick and Mac McDonald.

As I stared at the multi-mixer—not sure if I could handle its history, let alone make a thick shake—Irene explained the process. She demonstrated each step and then it was my turn. Should I pray to Ray and the McDonald brothers for help? I put the ingredients into a metal cup and placed it onto the spindle. I held my breath until the milk, ice-cream and flavoured colouring swirled prettily. But when I removed the cup I left the spindle switched on and so wore most of the chocolate shake on my new men's shirt. Unperturbed, Irene patiently went through the process again. After three hours I became an expert. Whenever the front counter was quiet,

I cleaned that five-spindle devil with a sanitised toothbrush until it shone like new. I wish I'd kept one of those multi-mixers for posterity, because they were decommissioned when the automatic shake machine arrived in the early 1990s.

The menu was simple back then, comprising only twelve items. I knew that if my training stayed on track and I successfully managed Shakes for three days, I would graduate to Fries. A small victory and a promotion within the week would be mine. My dexterity shone on French Fries—a standalone station that did not require a team effort, and one that, if it didn't operate at one hundred per cent, created chaos. Orders would quickly back up as most customers wanted fries with their meal. I had found my place of comfort.

Later in my career, if I needed some down time, that's where you'd find me—on Fries. No communication required. Only me and my salt shaker. Well, only me, the shaker and the buzzer that reminded me to 1) shake the fries every minute so they didn't stick together; 2) remove and drain them after three minutes and ten seconds so they weren't oily or burnt, and 3) every seven minutes discard old chips and start again, so orders were hot and fresh for every customer. But it was my place of calm without staff questions, customer demands or management decisions. Just the Fries and I.

Often, after my shift ended, I remained at the store to study the McDonald's manual and to view American training videos which were designated 'not to leave the store'. My favourite video was 'Opening the Restaurant'. The first scene was of a McDonald's store covered in snow, which was rare in downtown Melbourne. The American narrator detailed how the maintenance man should use a shovel to clear the snow from the roof and entrances. Maybe that's why early Australian stores were built with pitched roofs. The narrator's strong American drawl reminded me of the then popular TV shows *Dallas* and *Charlie's Angels*. And I always got a laugh out of selecting the option to switch the dialogue into Spanish.

After completing the individual station training I began learning to manage the shift. Throughout my career this remained a favourite part of the job; no day was the same and there were never enough hours to complete all the tasks required.

The area I found most difficult was called Production. The production manager, facing the customers over a stainless steel warming bin, tried to read customer's minds and imagine what they might purchase as they waited in the queue. They would then call out the type and amount of product to the kitchen staff to start preparation. Sometimes generalisations were helpful: if a group of Asian customers arrived we would drop (cook) a tray of 36 crumbed chicken and Filet-O-Fish pieces. Builders and labourers would channel Big Macs and Quarter-Pounders, which came without cheese in the 1980s. And if a busload of school children were spotted unloading in the car park the cheeseburgers and fries were at the ready.

The burgers were only kept in the warming bin for ten minutes so it was important not to waste any. The McFeast had a shorter lifespan because the lettuce and tomato combo remained fresh for only five minutes. With experience you got it right, though sometimes, completely wrong. I learnt very quickly that the back crew was much better at guessing customers' orders at different times of the day than me.

With friends I have often described working at McDonald's

as like school, except that you get paid. There are schedules, discipline, learning, mischief, friends, mentors, teachers and people who will you to succeed.

On one occasion a shift at Cheltenham was not going well when Charlie Bell, then Regional Manager, arrived unannounced with an entourage. Assessing the situation, he asked simply, 'Where would you like me?'

'The dining room please,' I gratefully replied. Charlie liked to catch McDonald's people 'doing it right' and on that day he stayed for a couple of hours until I had it right.

I learnt early that it was okay to accept help and to never feel embarrassed about needing that help.

Chapter 2

Silence is Golden

My training schedule stayed on track and five months later I proudly took delivery of a red 'Second Assistant Manager' name badge, and a wood laminate slat for the front counter announcing that 'Michele Layet' was the duty manager at South Oakleigh McDonald's. It didn't take me long to realise that some managers would slack off on their shifts and put someone else's name slat on the board so they'd get the blame if anyone complained. When I wised up to these shenanigans, my name slat came home with me after every shift. I know, I know, taking company property home was very serious, but it saved a lot of hassle with unscrupulous peers. Loving a challenge, I set myself a tight schedule to earn the next name badge, 'First Assistant', and then to reach my nirvana, 'Store Manager'.

The creators of the McDonald's training program really understood the power of levels and promotions to motivate people. Moving up through the ranks was a goal for most staff, and the public branding through badges meant everyone knew where they stood. By studying manuals, watching videos and completing work journals your efforts were recognised by your manager and you could then be sent off to sit exams or do the next course. Training managers from Head Office liked to drop in and do unannounced shift visits to check staff were on track with their work journals, and how you were running shifts. The usual path was from Trainee Crew, to Crew Member, Crew Trainer, Crew Chief, Trainee Manager, Second Assistant, First Assistant, and finally to Store Manager. Coming in where I did meant I missed all of the crew milestones within the ranking system, and was therefore doubly pleased when I earned each promotion.

A method of gauging a store's strengths and weaknesses was the Secret Customer Report compiled by an external reporting source. Once a week a person unknown to staff visited and filled in a detailed questionnaire scoring cleanliness, staff friendliness and product freshness from a customer's point of view. The requirements: hot food, friendly greetings and that well-known suggestive sell, 'Would you like fries with that?'

In the early days, there were no meal deals so suggestive selling was the sales tool employed. By encouraging the five thousand customers in our store each week to spend an extra $1 on top of the average of $5, we could add an extra $5,000 to our weekly sales. When a customer ordered a burger, fries, drink and dessert a deft manager could be heard asking, 'Would you like cookies with that?' to ensure full points were scored and an extra sale occurred.

The Secret Customer Report always named the manager on duty, hence the importance of those name slats. The results were posted to the store a couple of days later, and when the mail arrived all eyes were on the magic envelope. Only the store manager could open it and sometimes these reports mysteriously disappeared. State Management eventually wised up and requested duplicates be sent to head office.

Yes, it was a spying tool, but I always took pride in my shifts no matter who was watching, and viewed it as way to develop our ability to manage a business. My parents had instilled in me a desire to always meet my own high expectations, never mind anyone else's. McDonald's had a detailed system of checks and balances, reports, competitions and judging that would send any normal person insane. A checklist was even required to check off the checklists! The height of the lawn was a favourite inclusion, followed closely by the width of a tomato and the length of a frozen chip. In this business a ruler was a crucial management tool.

It was company policy to permanently move newly promoted managers to a higher sales restaurant, so that they could establish their authority without pressure from previous peers. Elsternwick was selected for me to practise my new-found skills on unfamiliar staff in a fresh environment. The beauty of Macca's means that any staff member can slot in at any store, any time. While there are some variations in store design, sales and equipment, the processes and systems are uniform, replicated exactly across all stores. And speaking of uniforms, after 14 months there still wasn't a female manager's outfit. Patience, Michele.

My nerves were jumping when I arrived at 11.30 am, half an hour early, for my first shift at Elsternwick. I reminded myself that the policy of always having two managers on duty for lunch and dinner shifts meant there should be plenty of time for the existing manager to give me a full induction to the store and the staff.

'Hi, my name's Michele, nice to meet you,' I approached

a man wearing the manager's uniform of a white Pelaco shirt, brown tie and dark brown pants with my hand outstretched.

Ignoring my handshake offer, he thrusted a set of keys at me and without even a 'hello', instructed me to 'get on the floor.' (It's not what you think — it means 'run the shift').

'I'll be downstairs,' he added as he started to walk away.

'Who are the front and back managers today?' I asked. With no name badge and no introduction, I didn't know what to call him.

'You're in charge; work it out,' he grunted as he piled up a tray with three pieces of fried chicken (there were no nuggets then) a Big Mac, Coke and a chocolate sundae.

No introduction, induction or store tour and a manager walking off the shift at lunchtime? I tried again. 'Who's working with me tonight?'

'Don't know.'

'Well, can you show me where the crew and managers rosters are kept? I tried to call yesterday but the phone was engaged for ages.' I tried to keep my tone pleasant.

'Check the cupboard above the desk,' he mumbled through a mouth stuffed with fries.

Before I had a chance to open the cupboard a crew member, Andrew, stuck his head around the corner. 'Michele, the bun delivery guy is at the front counter. He reckons a red Laser's in his way.' At least someone acknowledged me.

With my promotion and pay rise, I'd taken out a loan to buy a brand-new Ford Laser. At the time it was my pride and joy. I needed reliable transport because I had to get stock from other stores (not allowed now), do the banking (definitely not allowed now) and drive staff home late at night (not preferred these days). My 1967 Toyota Cortina, nicknamed Kevin, was not reliable for late-night shifts, early morning starts or, on reflection, anything. If night staff had needed a lift home, they had to push-start Kevin.

'Thanks. I'll move it and do a travel path. If you need a hand, call the other manager,' I said.

Andrew laughed at my irony, and continued filling up metal baskets with frozen fries.

A 'travel path' is the manager's walk to check all customer and staff areas, toilets, car park, dining room, stock room and the surrounding neighbourhood, including a walk around the block. This was very enticing, because we were expected to take these walks every thirty minutes; it was a chance for a cigarette and a break from the shift. It seems managers don't do regular travel paths now because many have given up smoking. I believe this has affected the block walk and observation of neighbourhood rubbish. Hear, hear, you say.

I was too late and the delivery guy had finished dumping multiple crates of buns around my car.

'You could have waited, mate.'

As he jumped into the truck I yelled, 'Hang on! Where's the invoice?'

My words were drowned out by his speedy departure. Great. Now I had no way to cross-check the delivery. The back door was already open so I dragged all the bun crates inside. Pulling out my compulsory mini-notepad from my shirt pocket, I made a note to remind the staff to keep the back door closed and locked at all times.

Staff name badges were a life saver. Perhaps they ought to be a standard item at schools, thirty-year reunions and even fiftieth birthday parties for those who are starting to forget things.

'Andrew,' I asked, 'did the bun guy leave a docket?'

'Sorry, I don't know. By the way, one of our full-timers called in sick and a customer reckons teachers have gone on strike.'

'Can you call someone to replace the shift?'

'Sure and I'll call a couple of others to help out,' Andrew nodded and picked up the phone.

We both knew the store would be overflowing with school kids, many of them casual employees of the store, unwilling to get behind the counter in front of their classmates. I headed downstairs to the basement and found the manager chatting up two female crew who'd just clocked on.

'Girls, could you please start now? It's about to get busy.'

'Sure,' they answered in unison as I walked back upstairs.

'Andrew, do you want me to work front or back?' I asked. While he was only crew level, I felt I could rely on him as a potential ally.

'Counter, please.'

I was relieved, because Andrew would have a better understanding of customer order patterns and be more proficient in the production role. My internal planning continued as I covered mental checklists.

'Andrew, we didn't get any Mac buns delivered. Have we enough for the lunch rush?'

'No, we've run out.'

The Big Mac bun can't be replaced by any other bun. It's not the sesame seeds; it's the three bread layers: crown, club, and heel.

'I'll call another store to borrow some,' I said, heading downstairs to get the manager to collect the buns. He was nowhere to be found so I asked one of the girls if they could pick up the Mac buns from our closest store.

'Sure,' she said. 'And Brendan's just left.'

'Who's Brendan?'

'The Manager.'

'Great.' I was too frantic to ask, or even wonder if this was normal behaviour for him.

The shift continued relentlessly. I had no toilet or cigarette breaks, no food, and certainly no time for that essential travel path. There wasn't even time to put my slat up or bring in the flags at dusk. Oh, for a visit from Head Office just to get some help.

Someone once told me a McDonald's shift should run like a well-orchestrated ballet. Throughout my shift I wondered what ballet they were thinking of as I seemed to be starring in the craziest madcap version of *The Nutcracker*.

At 4 pm the night manager did not show and Brendan was still AWOL. Finally around 10.30 pm they both arrived wearing silly grins and a festive air.

'You can do a lot pick-up now. I'll finish the shift,' Brendan ordered.

'Actually I reckon she should bring in the flags and fix up the dumpster,' the night manager slurred.

'Change of plans. Clean the loos and then you can go home,' Brendan announced.

I later learned they'd gone to the pub after deciding I needed to undergo a rite of passage.

As the derogatory commentary continued, I walked out

and sped off in my new car, relieved it didn't need a push start. When you make a dramatic exit it's imperative it goes smoothly. But silence is golden and can be quite powerful. When I walked out that night, no one knew what I thought or whether I would return. It had been a really tough shift and one of many difficult 'first days' on the job. It was also one of only two occasions in my career that a McDonald's shift brought me to tears.

Chapter 3

The Highway to Cheltenham

I returned the next day to work my rostered shift and fortunately it went without incident. Over the next few months I did my best to ignore Brendan and focused on completing my management modules so I could become a first assistant manager within the year.

During my 13 months at Elsternwick I developed a reputation for brevity, particularly with head office staff. I hated being interrupted when there was time-critical work to be done. As the nearest store to the McDonald's Victorian Head Office in the Cadbury Schweppes building on St Kilda Road, Elsternwick was always run to the highest standards as the show-off store.

One lunchtime, on an exceptionally busy day with a transport strike causing hordes of kids to skip school and visit our store, in walked American Founder Ray Kroc with about eight staffers. I was on front counter at the time, and took a double take when I saw him. *Crap*, I thought. *What a crazy time to arrive.*

'Hi, I'm Ray Kroc,' he said, holding out his hand.

'Hi, it's so good to meet you Sir, but I'm afraid I'm too busy to talk right now.' I could feel the shocked glares of my crew and the head office staffers, but with the barely controlled chaos swirling around me, I really couldn't afford the time. The dining room was completely full, and there was a crush of customers at the front counter.

As I started to walk away, I overheard him drawl to his neighbour, 'I like her.' With that he turned heel and went, with his minions tottering behind.

While driving home that night I wondered why nobody warned me. Usually if the bigwigs were out travelling, the drumbeat would go out as we'd ring ahead to the next store to warn them, especially if we were friendly with the managers. Maybe we were the first. As soon as they left I certainly jumped on the phone to warn South Oakleigh.

The Elsternwick store had the rare distinction of a window on the car park side so that customers could see us working in the kitchen. All kinds of people would stop to watch staff flipping burgers, so we always ensured it was spotless. Elsternwick had fry vats near the front counter and production was called from the front unlike most stores who called it from the back. The only disadvantage to this layout was that as a manager you had your back turned to the customers. But it was innovative because McDonald's did not want managers running production. It was meant to be a crew station.

My preferred shifts were opens or closes rather than the day shift from 12 pm to 8 pm. In the days before the breakfast menu, stores opened for business at the very civilized time of 10.30 am with staff starting an hour and a half earlier to prepare for customers. As manager I would catch up with the maintenance man who was in charge of cleaning and minor repairs around the store, and then enjoy a quick gossip and smoke with staff all whilst inside—before the smoking bans sent us outside. I'd then write up the crew roster, count the frequently used stock items, phone in the bun count, order the shake and sundae mix, put the tills out and count the float. As Elsternwick was a company store I also had to collate invoices, check time-cards and compare them to rostered hours before putting the invoices and cards in a red satchel to be collected weekly by Head Office. Once a month I would also read the gas meter, as most of our grills and cooking vats were run on gas not electricity like now.

My training continued as did my need to understand the unusual way this crew did things. On my first closing shift I noticed crew member Tony placed garbage bags on the stainless-steel benches and closed off the grill while we were still serving customers.

'What are you doing that for?' I asked him. 'It's still half an hour before we close.'

'It'll save time when the doors shut.'

'I don't think so.' And it looked ridiculous, let alone a waste of bags. 'Please remove the bags and just wipe the benches down later.'

Similar things occurred out the front. Andrew (the lovely young man from my first shift) had left napkins under the drink tower to mop up spills, emptied the ice container, removed the sundae topping canisters and lids, and taken the French fries racks to the back sink for the wash-up person to deal with very early.

'But how do we put toppings on sundaes?'

'Use the plastic spoons.'

'What if a customer wants ice in their beverage?'

'Tell them we've run out. They'll get over it.'

'Are you seriously suggesting we use tongs for fries just so we can wash the fry scoop earlier?'

And on it went. All these 'shortcuts' actually made the job harder. It drove me round the bend.

A few months later I had my first experience of terminating crew at Elsternwick. Unfortunately I had to let Tony (now known as Green Bags) and the ever-popular Andrew go after several verbal and written warnings about various misdemeanours had failed to modify their behaviour. Andrew was constantly late for work, prone to telling senior managers how to do their jobs and often called in sick when we knew he was at the snow. But he was still one of the nicest crew members I worked with. Tony kept leaving shifts without notifying a manager, would smoke outside when it wasn't his break-time, and regularly ate food without paying for it. He also kept swapping into shifts that he hadn't been trained for. I sacked them both on the same shift after we'd closed the store at 11 pm. Understandably upset, they took off without finishing their shifts. I had to do the grill close and front close on my own—an additional three hours work—but at least the wash-up person was there to assist.

Close normally took one and a half hours, and then I did my management close duties, so I got home at 3 am, about four hours after shutting the store. When I arrived at my house there were two sheepish crew waiting outside to apologise for their poor behaviour. As they were armed with a bottle of Scotch I forgave them, but I did not reinstate them.

About six months into my time at Elsternwick the store was flagged to be sold by the company to become a franchisee store. I was informed I would be staying at Elsternwick and was initially devastated I would not be continuing with the McDonald's Corporation.

I arranged to meet with the incumbent franchisee, who as Company accountant signed my monthly salary cheques. Neither of us was impressed with the other and so I decided to look for employment elsewhere. (His son Adam Kelly now runs many stores including the store I always had my eye on to purchase one day—the coveted company store Prahran.)

I was interviewed by Denny's Diner for a position as a trainee manager and was offered a job at their first 24-hour store, which was due to open soon on Nepean Highway Moorabbin. I tendered my resignation from McDonald's Elsternwick in September 1983, enjoyed a few weeks off, and then started getting back into work mode. While I was waiting to commence at Denny's, a swing (casual) manager at Elsternwick recommended me to a franchisee who was about to purchase a second store and desperately needed a first assistant.

Apparently I'd developed a reputation as a good shift manager, and had helped Elsternwick improve their Full Field (McDonald's annual assessment rating) results considerably. Tony Wither already owned Cheltenham and due to his new purchase of the South Oakleigh store needed to hire managers quickly. He was transferring his Cheltenham manager to South Oakleigh, thus creating a vacancy at Cheltenham. Cheltenham had just failed their Full Field test in 1983, and Tony was worried about losing his franchisee licence.

I met with the Cheltenham Store Manager at the Mentone Hub Motel. It felt very secretive. They offered me the first assistant position immediately and so I asked them for a few days to consider my options. When I contacted Denny's the next day to check what the trainee manager salary was, they refused to confirm it. Instead they now wanted to put me on a lower starting wage and make the manager salary dependant on my personal progress and dedication to my training schedule. I thought we'd agreed on all of that at the interview. Doubts about working for them plagued my mind and so I decided to accept the position at Macca's Cheltenham as first assistant. I got along so well with Tony Wither I stayed working for him for eight years until I moved to South Australia.

Chapter 4

The True Meaning of PC

'Any distinguishing features?' asked the sergeant.
'He's six feet tall, with bright red hair, a yellow suit and big feet.'

Every year during the late summer Orientation Week university students held scavenger hunts and the Ronald McDonald statue was a coveted trophy. A couple of weeks after his 1984 abduction from the Cheltenham store the police called.

'We've located Ronald directing traffic at the Moorabbin airport. Can someone please collect him?'

To keep him safe from future travels, upon his return we placed him inside the store near the front counter.

In the 1980s the term PC referred to police constables on a television show called *The Bill*. Like the fictional UK cops, the local police and fire brigade proved very important to my wellbeing as a McDonald's employee.

After night shifts, around 2 am, with a couple of staff waiting for lifts home in my new red Laser, we'd take the day's earnings to a night safe at the local bank. Today, McDonald's has armed escorts of burly guards driving vans and standing watch, but back then, the money was kept in brown, fake-leather, key-locked wallets. If we were robbed, the thief would only need a pair of sharp scissors. Once, after an extremely busy McHappy Day, I was nervous about the banking and rang the local police to escort me, which they organised without question. Those were the days when the only PC I cared about served the local community.

Just before I started working at McDonald's South Oakleigh the store had been robbed. (During my initial training I learnt the difference between being robbed and burgled—a robbery involves people, while a burglary happens when no one is home.) The manager, Mike Goodluck, and two staff members had tried to escape on their bikes, but the thieves caught up to them and hauled them back inside. While waiting for the safe's time delay mechanism to operate, the balaclava-clad bandits locked the crew in the walk-in fridge and then marched Mike outside and forced him to lie face-down in the neighbouring paddock with two pistols pointed at his head. Apparently they were concerned passers-by might be suspicious at movement inside the store at 2 am. After the thirty minute delay passed, Mike opened the safe and handed over $2,000, before being locked in the fridge with his crew, who were jumping up and down to keep warm. Unwittingly the thieves also took a green dye bomb designed to stain the money and make it useless.

Soon after the robbers made their getaway in Mike's vivid-yellow Ford Cortina, Mike and crew managed to escape from the walk-in; they were cold but safe. About a week later the robbers rang the store to kindly inform the shift manager that they'd left the Cortina half a mile south of the Jordanville Railway Station. When Mike came to work for the closing shift that night, he found the police waiting for him.

'Mike Goodluck, we'd like to ask you a few questions about the robbery last week.'

Once at the station, they began firing questions at him, just like in the movies. 'Robbers don't give back stolen cars. You know them, don't you? Robbers aren't nice people who treat you like a friend while they're holding you up. Are you related to them in any way?'

Only when the thieves were caught a few hours later, while he was still being questioned, did they conclude he was not involved in the heist. Mike and I still enjoy a laugh over that situation. Mike and his wife, Bergs, now own four McDonald's franchises.

After that, floor safes were replaced with stand-alone units so managers could hand money over immediately. No more tick-tock of the safe clock as it counted down the regulatory thirty minutes to automatic opening, or the fear of a forced safe opening or the mess of an 80s tie-dye look marking the notes for police identification.

Once my franchisee had a call from an attendant at the neighbouring petrol station suggesting a burglary may have occurred at our store. Worried, the franchisee rang me and asked me to call into the store. When I arrived there, alone late at night, I found the safe—still locked and full of cash—in the middle of the car park.

Over the years, one incident became folklore. A guy tried to break into a store from the roof via the grill stack (which was a metal chimney) and got stuck. His feet were firmly planted on an unused grill while the rest of his body was stuck up the stack like a chimney sweep. Prior to the arrival of the fire brigade to cut him out, staff turned on the grill to heat up the situation a little.

Michele Layet

'Maybe he's got cold feet.'

People often question why McDonald's managers offer discounted food to uniformed police officers. There are many reasons: to encourage their visible presence which enhances security; to take away the guy passed out on the floor; to warn off angry customers who yell and spit at staff because breakfast has finished; or to deal with opposing gangs fighting in the car park. Or they might be handy to write up four missing pale pink dining-room chairs for an insurance claim. (Where *was* the manager that night?) Having police around also provides a general deterrent to unacceptable behaviour, particularly in the car park when they eat their meals in the divvy (divisional) van.

Phone calls to the police station were most frequent during the eight years I worked at McDonald's Cheltenham—I found myself calling them at least twice a week. There were several unrelated events: a lady drove through our fence when she thought she was in reverse. A white Toyota crashed straight off the Nepean Highway into our playground, bringing a whole new meaning to the concept of 'drive-thru', and narrowly missing a child. One evening a group of regular customers on a buck's night ran around the dining room naked. We didn't Tweet, Instagram or Facebook their image. Those tools were not yet invented. We didn't even call the police on that occasion; we just locked the four dining room doors and let them out later when they'd settled down.

On 22nd October 1984 a police officer on foot patrol at Southland shopping centre noticed thick, black smoke billowing from the Cheltenham store and notified emergency services. On the way to a managers meeting at noon that day I heard the lead news item on the car radio. 'A fire has destroyed a McDonald's store in Cheltenham.' The previous night's shift had been mine. I couldn't help questioning myself—had all the equipment been turned off?

When I arrived the store was smouldering and water cascaded out of the dining room doors. Fire hoses were snaked over the outside tiled area and the crew were waving despondently to me from the Red Rattler, the party train carriage, which was miraculously untouched. Charcoal was all I could see inside the now blackened building; there were no happy reds and yellows.

'When did it happen? Is everyone ok?' I asked, afraid of the answer. But the fire had started at 10am and everyone was safe. It transpired that a fry vat had caught alight and the little gas fire-retardant nozzle that should have extinguished the flames was pointed up the stack not down towards the oil. The system had failed, not me. This was not a good omen for the first day of Fire Prevention Week.

Once the firemen had extinguished the flames, they relaxed in the unharmed dining room drinking coffee. But unbeknown to them the fire had escaped into the pitched roof. A trader from the Southland photography shop saw the store roof suddenly burst into flames and alerted the crew and firemen who bolted back to the job, wearing oxygen masks.

Only three items survived the blaze; the train carriage, my manager-on-duty sign 'Michele Layet' and amazingly, the Ronald statue, completely unscathed. The name badge and statue were carefully removed from the wreckage and put into my friend Simonne's car. A fellow manager and close friend, she had a powder blue BMW with a sun roof, so Ronald was placed vertically with his head poking out of the sunroof. As we drove home along Nepean Highway, people tooted and waved acknowledging the world's most famous clown as he fled to safety. Simonne looked after him for a couple of weeks and during that time he went everywhere with her. She showed us photos of him playing tennis, relaxing on a banana lounge in her garden, and basking in the sun on trips to Dendy Beach. She posted these photos to our boss and franchisee Tony, (in an actual envelope, as there was no email or internet then) with regular updates of Ronald's happy travels.

Tony, a train enthusiast, eventually demanded Ronald's return, planning to put him inside the train carriage where we held birthday parties. Ronald was proudly displayed in his new environment and when the store was rebuilt he did not return to the front counter area but remained in the train carriage greeting thousands of rowdy party kids over the years.

During the two months the Cheltenham store was being rebuilt, Tony and I were keen to keep the crew together, as we'd built a wonderful team in the past year. Under the franchisee insurance policy, all staff pays for full-time and casual were covered for about eight weeks. This was another of Tony's initiatives when he was head of the Franchisee Insurance Committee. Previously only full-time staff were covered, and he brought in coverage for casuals as well. He had us fundraise for local welfare and charity organisations, help the Cheltenham Rotary Club raise funds for a water tank in Thailand, and support the parade for Victoria's 150th Celebrations on the 19th of November 1984. It seemed we were back at work in no time when the store reopened on 19th December.

So I'd like to keep the term PC for our wonderful police constables and find another term for political correctness.

Chapter 5

Would You Like a Stat With That?

Almost midnight. 'It can't be time to get up,' I groaned as I dragged myself out of a dream. It was Month End, which brought the onerous task of the stock count and Statistical Report. At the end of trade on the last day of each month, all across Australia an army of McDonald's store managers prepared to count everything from sugar packets to plastic dining room trays to foil ashtrays and everything in between. At least the ashtrays were phased out when indoor restaurants in South Australia became non-smoking in 1999.

It was quiet and pitch black outside as I sat in my car warming up the engine and willing the heater to work. At 1 am there was almost no traffic as I eased out onto the road, and when I neared the unlit Cheltenham store in 1987 it stood like a giant cardboard cut-out, a silhouette against the night sky.

I was eager to get started but security protocol dictated that I park near the main entrance and wait for the cleaner to arrive. The position of the car was to ensure a quick getaway should there be any trouble. The cleaner would provide extra security for me to enter the building. There was comfort in having another human around at those early starts, but on this occasion I waited more than thirty minutes for the cleaner to show before deciding to enter the store alone.

I switched on my car's high beam to check the immediate area. It would have been nice if staff had left at least one light on, but a manager, heavily engaged with the cost-saving chapter of her Management Development Program (MDP), had instructed the crew via her Equipment Fire-up Schedule (listing the timing for powering equipment on and off during the day) that all lights should be snuffed out at close. Depending on the zeal of the manager, there might be several dollar-saving projects going on at any one time. There were cash-register competitions, less-than-one-per-cent-targets, zero-cash-sheet-and-float discrepancy, and even reduced-garbage-bag-usage competitions (with the instruction that bags must be filled to at least 75% capacity before being changed). McDonald's managers are generally very competitive by nature and so these in-store undertakings were well-received.

Unable to spot any lurking strangers, I locked my car and headed quickly into the store. Flailing around in the dark, I found the light switch and lit up the entire front counter. Getting my priorities right, I put the coffee on first. While I was gathering my paperwork, the cleaner arrived and tip-toed straight to the dining room to avoid the 'You're forty-five minutes late,' conversation.

End-of-Month Counts, usually performed by senior managers, meant casual clothes, no customers and no staff to deal with. When the count was finally and exhaustively completed, I'd return home to sleep for the day.

But before that, I had just eight hours to count stock in the freezer, fridge, kitchen, dining room cupboards, front counter, stock room, uniform and party cupboards, write up a statement of inventory, and report to head office on sales figures, customer counts and promotional sales numbers. This was all manually assessed, as there were no fax lines or direct computer links in the 1980s. Also on the to-do list was checking store transfers and delivery invoices and reading the gas and electricity meters.

For accuracy the aim was to finish before the opening crew arrived and commenced stocking the front counter and kitchen areas. Stock levels were allowed to drop prior to the end-of-month count to save time. Leading up to the count it was also ideal to minimize open stock in cupboards, shelves and stock areas.

I always commenced my stocktake at front counter. I pulled half-used sleeves of small cups, lids, coffee stirrers and serviettes out of the cupboards, tidied the under-counter holding areas and sorted shake and sundae toppings and nugget sauces before putting the pen to my count sheet.

Next I estimated the shake and sundae mix in the machine hoppers before heading to the French Fries station. I cleaned out the cupboard to be salt free and estimated the number of small fry bags remaining in a box of 4000, and followed up with an accurate count of medium and large fry boxes. I needed a ladder to count the burger boxes, wraps and nugget boxes stacked on the kitchen shelves in the grill area.

Moving on I tackled the walk-in fridge, exchanging my pen for a pencil, as pens do not work well at minus 18. Every manager has their own system but to make the count more accurate I always tidied up first. I rotated all the items, checked dates, threw out empty boxes and ensured the use-by dates were facing outwards. I methodically worked from front to back, left to right and top to bottom, cursing the increase in variety of products as the years passed.

After an hour in the freezer I was well-awake but despite delivery truck gloves my hands were still freezing. The light globe blew and I grabbed another one to replace it. It was 'interesting' standing on a chair in the dark trying to manoeuvre a torch (with dodgy batteries) in one bear-like hand, and a globe in the other.

Because the main delivery had arrived the previous day, the freezer was depressingly full. I stood and faced 192 boxes of frozen fries, 48 boxes of 10:1 meat (10 patties to the pound, used in the Big Mac, Cheeseburger and Junior burger) and 24 boxes of 4:1 (they're the quarter-pounder patties and, logically, four to a pound in weight). I took a deep breath and commenced the count.

The crew from the night before had opened more than one box of the same product so each individual patty from three opened boxes had to be counted. Next on the list were filet (fish) pieces and apple pies which had been placed up high on top of the nugget boxes by some giant crew person. Every few minutes I had to go out of the freezer to warm up. The neat stacks of eight boxes to a row stacked eight boxes high had a six inch gap all around for circulation. Don't drift off here—you may learn something about refrigeration. For instance, crumbed items such as filets and nuggets need to be in the coldest section of the fridge, that is, not near the door. The apple pies in particular are very sensitive to increases in temperature and will stick together if not stored at the back. The take-away lesson here is that at home, it is best not to put your milk carton in the fridge door because it is the warmest section of your fridge. The last items I counted were ice-cream cakes and chicken patties.

As I left the walk-in I gathered up two empty six-pack nugget containers, along with empty sachets of sweet and sour, the most popular sauce. Obviously these remains from an illicit snack enjoyed by staff doing stock-up were not listed as sold, nor marked off the waste sheet or staff-meals sheet. You'd think the fridge would be the last place you'd want to snack in, but it was the best place to minimise the chance of being caught eating on the job.

My final destination was the stock room, left until last so that if I wasn't finished when the crew arrived at 9 am, they could remove stock and let me know what they'd taken. On reflection, I now realise that no matter how many stores I worked at, I always did the EOM count in the same order, regardless of design changes over the years.

Ideally staff used all items in one box before opening another, but it was annoyingly common to find multiple opened boxes of the same thing. This time I found three opened boxes of medium cups, two opened sleeves of Cheeseburger wraps and three boxes of opened Sweet and Sour sauces. It would have been so easy to tally two full boxes, and then count the sleeves of cups in the open one. Instead I had to pull out all the sleeves from the three opened boxes, and count the sleeves individually. And of course, those boxes were on the highest shelf.

Finally I put my clipboard down, tidied up, and rotated the

stock, with the oldest dates (soonest to expire) at the front. Which was how everything was supposed to be stored when it was first delivered but sometimes the crew unloading the delivery would, for ease, put the new delivery in front of the older product.

When I completed all the counting, I tallied up all the figures, and calculated the amount of stock used compared to what was reported as used according to the point of sale (POS) figures. But never did the two match. The Big Mac chant tells you that the burger contains (all together now): two all-beef patties, special sauce, lettuce, cheese, pickles, onions, on a sesame-seed bun. Sounds simple doesn't it? Two beef patties, then one of everything else, but what if extra cheese was added? Or if someone didn't like the pickle? We all know the stories about customers throwing unwanted pickle onto the ceiling— far better to ask for your burger without it.

The actual Apple Pies used versus sold were always in the store's favour. They were listed on the register at the bottom and were the last thing packed (remember? Desserts go in last), so they were sometimes forgotten. The worst offender for discrepancies between actual usage versus POS usage was Chicken Nuggets, followed closely by cheese slices and the regular buns used for Cheeseburgers, Junior Burgers and Filet-O-Fish. Filet-O-Fish pieces usually matched as they were not a high theft item like nuggets, Cheeseburgers and Happy Meals.

When actual figures did not match expected figures by more than 1% I would need to implement several actions, including a recount of relevant products, rechecking of deliveries received and transfer dockets between stores, as well as a recount of the staff-meals sheet and waste sheet records for the whole month.

Before computer data entry, transfer dockets were the worst part of EOM. They were often left in manager's cars, not picked up when product was collected, lost, misplaced or they were incorrectly priced. Transfers were added up manually and hand-written, leaving the contents of the dockets up to some interpretation.

Waste was counted every day after the lunch, afternoon and dinner shifts. Managers or senior staff recorded food that was thrown away, out of date, dropped on the floor, over/under cooked or returned from customers who changed their orders. Before the food preparation system 'Made for You' (MFY) was invented, this was a cumbersome, boring task because more completed product was required to fill the holding bins. We had two bins: one for completed products and countable items, ie a Big Mac in a box or a cheese slice that had fallen on the floor, and another for coffee granules as they could be composted. Three times each day we counted foam boxes, straws, and half-filled cups of shake and soft drinks and take-out bags. I avoided this task wherever possible, leaving senior crew to count waste on my shifts. MFY certainly decreased completed waste but did not stop idiots who threw coffee grains in the wrong bin mixed up with buns, lettuce and too soft, soft-serve cones. Digging through all of that to separate countable items from old coffee grains was disgusting.

On another clipboard staff meals were recorded during shifts. Managers, myself included, were the worst offenders in terms of accuracy. There were coffees, soft drinks (not orange juice because of the high cost, the same for chicken), a burger grabbed quickly between rushes or perhaps some nuggets and sauce sitting in the office and shared by all. Management didn't object to staff meals but those meals did need to be recorded. Unless crew sneaked food on their travel paths in the grounds, in the freezer or walk-in fridge, or gave it away to friends (otherwise known as theft), they paid at the counter and it was tracked. The crew uniform then did not have pockets and there was nowhere for hands, money or food to be hidden. We had a saying: if you have time to lean you have time to clean. Uniforms have pockets now, for the mobile phone, which is a great shame in my opinion.

The time required to complete the physical count has increased over the years due to the increasing number of items we sell, but the computer has replaced manual calculations saving time and increasing accuracy.

As my eight-hour marathon came to an end and the early crew wandered in, I patted myself on the back. Ideally the count needed to be completed prior to the store opening so errors could be resolved. With the introduction of a breakfast menu in late 1989 and consequently earlier and longer trading hours this was not always possible, but I usually finished on time.

At 9 am I inhaled a last coffee as I gathered my reams of paperwork. Note to self: mark off one packet of coffee, one coffee cup, one stirrer and two-and-a-half packets of sugar.

Chapter 6

The Dress Rehearsal

The look, feel, and quality of food at McDonald's worldwide ought to be uniform no matter where you are enjoying your Big Mac, Filet-O-Fish or Junior Burger. The reason for this is the 'Full Field' process. Every eighteen months McDonald's stores were intensively assessed over three days by a consultant from McDonald's head office to ensure that prescribed ways of operating were adhered to. It was a no-holds-barred inspection of every detail of the store's operation, from the correct number of pickles on burgers, stopwatch measurements of speed of service, to the presence of even a skerrick of chewing gum under dining room tables. For crew, managers and franchisees receiving an excellent report after these visits from head office was the holy grail of their business, governing store acquisitions, pay rises and reputation. They generated almost certifiable behaviour in those involved, and often sent me around the bend with all the sleepless nights working long hours.

Usually the franchisee is in charge of preparation for the Full Field Process, but Tony was in desperate need of a holiday and as General Manager I was the obvious choice in 1987. Not knowing quite what I'd signed up for, I agreed to run the show.

The first date would be pre-planned but the follow-up visit was unannounced and occurred between 30 and 90 days from the first assessment. This allowed the store time to fix any problems, book tradesmen to complete technical jobs and to gloat about previous successes before being subjected to the process all over again.

Areas of examination were 'Quality', 'Service' and 'Cleanliness' (Q.S.C), with 'Value' added later as an additional criterion. Possible scores for each area were A, B, C or Fail. Anyone with aspirations of becoming a multi-store owner needed to aim for a triple A rating.

A couple of months prior to a diarised visit, store managers distributed the Full Field Checklist—thirty pages in triplicate—to three carefully selected and auditioned staff members to head up each category of Q.S.C. These people were chosen for their willingness and ability to get jobs done without supervision, work extra hours without pay, and be assertive enough to manage both the crew and the franchisee. They in turn auditioned their own teams based on similar criteria, and then the dress rehearsal commenced.

The bulk of the 'Quality' score was given on the actual day of testing. Points were awarded on complete McDonald's products: what the customer on the day of the test received and ate, rather than the quality of individual ingredients. The other categories relied on practise and pre-planning. Managers would spend many a Friday night coaching the crew to centre the pickles, salt the fries from left to right, and apply the correct number of shots of ketchup to a burger. But despite this effort, on first nights I'd watch helplessly as experienced crew poured ketchup on a Filet-O-Fish, dressed (that's the term for putting stuff on your burgers) burnt buns and put Big Macs upside down in their boxes. Ah, there's nothing like examination pressure to put you off your game.

The night before the Full Field we'd scrutinised the use-by dates of all products. Products within their expiry date range but not always used in date order were removed from the store temporarily. Points would be deducted for such disregard. As frozen goods could not be taken home for those three days, they were temporarily shipped to a nearby McDonald's. Fifteen-litre boxes of Coca Cola and sachets of Vegemite followed opened bags of chocolate topping into a manager's car. When breakfasts first commenced the Vegemite sachets came in boxes of 400—nearly a two-year supply and well beyond the four month expiry date.

'Maybe you could share a box with another store,' a consultant once suggested as he walked to my dumpster and threw out 299 sachets. On average only one sachet per day was consumed so the use-by date always came and went long before there was any chance to get through the supply. I still have sachets from 1993 in my cupboard at home.

It was vital to maintain strong relationships with suppliers and local traders. Sometimes tomatoes were the wrong colour or size so we would make a quick trip to the greengrocer. Or a phoned-in milk order was wrong and my milkman would rectify and re-deliver immediately. And when the ice machine broke down once during a Full Field we asked the nearby garage to ship in extra bags of ice from their supplier at cost. This is not allowed now, unless it is food grade—obviously cooling your drink in the days of grabbing ice out of the laundry tub at parties was a highly dangerous activity. No wonder we all felt sick with nerves the next day. The size and shape of ice cubes was a scored 'Quality' item in the Full Field.

The 'Service' score was the people's vote and therefore the subjective category. The rostering manager together with the service manager drew up the schedule early, ensuring the best crew were available. Heaps of additional staff were rostered on for the three days of the initial visit: a dining room person who cleared tables, changed bins and mopped floors, as well as a hostess with balloon skills dedicated solely to the role of customer care on a busy Friday night. And a couple of extra cash registers were dusted off and manned to speed up order times.

Tick-tock. We started checking our own watches as we prepared for timed service assessment of how long customers spent in a queue, time at the counter, and the time it took us to assemble an order.

Service meetings were conducted and extra training provided so that everyone was up to speed enabling the chosen ones to practise together as a team leading up to the opening night. We then had to make it less obvious that hordes of extra staff had been engaged for the test. One item on the Full Field Checklist required the inspector to 'check previous roster for similar volume over past 30 days'. Our Full Field roster therefore had to appear to be just another ordinary weekend of superior service. And so the service manager did what any self-respecting burning-to-slay-all-competitors soul would do: doctor the previous month's roster to match the hours used over the test period.

Newer crew were the best choice for Full Fields. The fresh faces hadn't learnt any bad habits or shortcuts and were eager to do their best—so all the steps taught would be executed in their correct order.

The service manager lectured staff on how their hair should look: 'neat and tidy, representative of the customers they were serving, and of natural colour' according to the policy. I'd be surprised if any of us can remember our natural hair colour. All of the dress rules applied to both sexes and included a no-earrings policy. No fake nails either because they could, and sometimes did, fall into the food.

Finally this was an opportunity for new uniforms to be distributed and name badges updated. Staff members who continually forgot their name badges or mischievously borrowed someone else's would once again be correctly 'named'. The back-up badges—Barney, Wilma and Fred, kept in a drawer for when crew forgot theirs—were given a three-day rest. Wearing these badges was supposed to be embarrassing but they often became sought-after tokens of disobedience.

If an 'A' was to be achieved in 'Cleanliness', it would need a willingness from the franchisee to spend money. The manager might have to beg a little. The one-sided conversation would sometimes go like this:

'We must re-cover the dining room chairs that are torn or have graffiti on them. That's cheap at about $750 for the lot,' I'd say to my franchisee, while thinking, *an 'A' is the golden chalice.*

'Can we paint the store? It will only cost about $4,000.' *If we get an 'A' I can work at Head Office.*

'What about new asphalt in the car park? That's $8,000.' *If we get three 'A's you may get a second store.*

To save money once, when I was still the Store Manager at Cheltenham, I took one of the managers up on the roof with me, tied a rope onto him, and supported him while he climbed down onto the pitched section of the roof to change the fluorescent lights under the beams. Much cheaper and quicker than getting an electrician in. On that same roof we later nailed fishing wire to prevent pigeons landing and pooing everywhere. This was in the 1980s, before OH&S really existed. Oh, the things we did to save money and achieve the top score!

Usually, the franchisee would deny most financial requests which meant managers and crew had to don overalls and get physical. We painted the flagpoles, staffroom and office areas. Outdoor areas were steam cleaned with a hired high-pressure machine, and the car park was scrubbed. Dints in the menu board were filled with Tippex and some guys from the local council were paid in food to put asphalt in the car park potholes. The night before the visit a team of volunteers met at the store after closing and started scrubbing everything in sight. Now that most stores are open twenty-four hours, that would be nearly impossible. Over the years I learnt to work smarter not harder but at least the long nights were a chance to bond over loud music and pizzas, which we'd ordered in so as not to dirty the kitchen.

My responsibility while manager at Cheltenham was always the walk-in fridge. I would clean the condensers, the floor, shelving and tiles. Next, I'd get up a ladder and scrub the entire store ceiling. Later, as a franchisee, older and less energetic, I put myself down to do the dining room tables; a slightly smaller job. I scraped off the chewy beneath table tops and scrubbed the stainless steel bases. This onerous task could take up to sixteen hours to complete properly depending on the number of tables.

In 1984, the year of the Cheltenham fire, we didn't get to benefit from all of our intense planning and hard work when the store burnt down just one week prior to the consultant's announced visit. Only the previous week I'd had the fire company in to service all the fire equipment in preparation for the Full Field. In a somewhat grim comedy of errors the nozzles in the stacks were left pointing up, rather than down on the oil. When the automatic sprinkler system failed, the manager broke the glass to set off the manual system—this failed—and the extinguisher near the fry vat jammed and failed as well.

When an insurance company representing McDonald's took Fire Fighting Enterprises to court seven years later, suing them for the rebuild cost of $1.1 million, the much-hated Full Field forms that had been painstakingly completed in triplicate became vital evidence. As an added bonus, when the store was rebuilt we scored an 'A' for cleanliness because everything was new. Even the washing machine—used to launder cleaning cloths used in the kitchen, dining room and for maintenance—got two points. We'd previously lost points for small chips in the paintwork and had been known to get busy with a bottle of Tippex to colour in dints and scratches on Ronald McDonald, the washing machine and the white fibreglass menu boards. It turns out Tippex works really well on fibreglass.

So, with the props and costumes at the ready, the stage set and the script fully rehearsed, it was curtain time.

Chapter 7

Showtime

I'd just finished brewing a pot of coffee when the head office consultant arrived at 8 am on a summer's day in 1987.

'Go about your business as usual and forget I'm here,' Gerrie said, unaware that I'd been at the store all night and had raced back only minutes earlier after showering at a friend's house nearby. 'I'm sure the day will run smoothly; I'm not here to catch you doing anything wrong.'

For a moment I almost believed her, but with her pen poised above her clipboard, stopwatch in hand and flinty eyes already scanning for chipped kitchen tiles, carbon-encrusted spatulas or incorrect cash-safety procedures, I knew what lay behind those words. I poured us both a coffee and introduced her to the day manager and a couple of key crew who looked like they were experiencing deer-in-headlights syndrome as they self-consciously went about their daily tasks.

To ensure minimal disruption for customers, the Full Field process began well before the store opened at 10:30 am. Gerrie inspected the cleanliness of the kitchen and service areas, performed a few calibrations and checked crew set-up procedures while I hovered nearby. In the front area we checked for a frozen ice-block in the milk dispenser, that the dining room trays were spotless and, most importantly, that the sundae topping heaters were on. Cool 'hot' fudge on a sundae was unacceptable. Gerrie checked out the back for tomato quality, that the wall-freezer was stocked and that the nugget packets and Filet-O-Fish portions were stacked neatly. For each item on the Full Field checklist she would make her inspection, award or detract points, and calculate a score. This section went well and we received full marks.

It was usual procedure for the consultant to check some detailed cleaning first. Before any mishaps or messes occurred I pulled down the roof ladder and climbed into the ceiling space with Gerrie right behind me. Of course the roof space light bulb had burnt out, so it was back down to locate a long-unused torch. Frustrated, I sent a manager to buy batteries from the petrol station and I left a note for the maintenance man to change that bulb.

While waiting for the batteries I suggested checking the toilets. Gerrie descended from the ceiling and we marched to the toilets to inspect the grout between the tiles and the cleanliness of the s-bend. Those items passed, but alas the mirrors were scratched and points were deducted.

With the rejuvenated torch we headed back up the ladder to check the exhaust fans (used to extract heat and grease from the grills).

All day the judging shifted from quality control, to service, to cleanliness and back again. We moved to the front counter area, ready to check the calibration of the milk dispenser, Coke syrup-to-soda ratio, shake syrup quantity and sundae topping volumes. I trotted off to retrieve the plastic calibration measuring cup I'd used the night before, but it was nowhere to be found. Mystified and mumbling obscenities, I sent a crew member to drive to a nearby store to borrow their calibration kit.

No matter how well prepared we were, the weirdest things occurred all day. I felt like I was watching the *Phantom of the Opera* trying to swing about, only without the chandelier.

In the back area, the grills were on wheels to allow for cleaning and I pulled them out and shone the torch up the exhaust hoods while the consultant lay on the floor to ensure that it was spotless under the back sink. Together we measured ice-cubes and lifted the Big Mac toaster to check for runaway sesame seeds.

On arrival of the calibration kit the next section of the 'Quality' standards commenced. Each dispenser on the dress bench (where toasted buns were placed) had a separate lever that released an exact amount of mustard, ketchup and Mac sauce. The dollops were checked in a measuring cup and recorded in triplicate.

Next, armed with a clipboard each and a stopwatch to record lunch service times, Gerrie and I put the dining room under the microscope. Friendliness of the staff and accuracy of the six-step service was rated. In order of importance ranked: the greeting, order-taking, the all-important suggestive sell, taking money and assembling the meal. The latter must be done in the right order: cold items first, burgers and fries in the middle and sundaes and apple-pies last. Then finally 'Hope you enjoy your meal, please come again'.

All of this was not complicated under normal circumstances but on testing days even the best staff buckled under the pressure. Suggestive selling was forgotten and less ice than prescribed was scooped into paper cups. 'Fill to the top of the M on the cup,' I wanted to scream! One customer came to the counter from the dining room after waiting several minutes for a Filet-O-Fish.

'Are you bloody catching the fish or what?' he yelled, peering into the kitchen. An extra minute is a long time when you're hungry.

Timing of service was repeated for the dinner rush and snack time. I cringed often throughout the day as I witnessed incorrect drinks poured, take away orders put on dining room trays and customers returning for missing nugget sauces. Eager to meet the 90 second time criteria, staff resorted to stealing other staff's ordered product instead of waiting for their own.

Tick-tock. Your 90 seconds is up.

You'd know your local Macca's was in the throes of a Full Field if you saw a nervous manager seated in the dining room with a clipboard, pen and a stopwatch next to a person dressed like an undertaker.

Throughout the visit, like a mashed-up ventriloquist, Marcel Marceau and Mr Bean all in one, I instructed my managers on the sly, miming hints and hissing reminders to do that travel path. It wasn't unusual during scoring for a staff member to walk off in a flood of tears, and it usually took some placation to convince them that we would, repeat would, get good scores and that even if we didn't, it wasn't their fault.

We moved on to testing the menu items, which involved judging cooked products. Gerrie mimicked a customer and ordered food for two. Carrying a tray of food each to the dining room the 'completed product section' began. Points were heavily weighted here because this was, in the end, what the customer purchased, ate and decided whether to come back for. As they say, the proof was in the pudding, or in this case, the Big Mac.

I felt the eyes of the whole crew watching as Gerrie unwrapped her Big Mac. I frowned as I saw a messy burger with the lettuce sliding off sideways, and the meat patties had not been seasoned with salt and pepper.

'It's only their nerves,' I said, as she tasted her burger.

'Mmm,' she replied, chewing thoughtfully. 'There are an awful lot of short fries in this pack.'

Throughout the day I made similar excuses as all logic failed the crew.

'I'll just get you another sweet and sour sauce for your nine pack of nuggets.' My voice raised a notch with each mistake. I sounded desperate because I was.

Despite glitches, the scoring continued relentlessly. The temperature of various food items was checked with a thermometer and remnants of cheese slice evident on a burger wrapper were noted. Amounts of ketchup and other condiments on burgers were checked against the prescribed dollop size.

As simple as a box of French Fries looks to the untrained eye, there is a whole semi-science behind it. The world-famous French Fries must sit within strict parameters. They must be not mealy (undercooked) and must have the correct ratio of long fry strands in a serve. And they must be kept hot within their regulatory seven-minute holding time. This is all trickier than it sounds. If a box of frozen fries was dropped from waist height when unloaded from a delivery truck, the fries would break. When cooked there would be a disproportionate number of short strands which meant more fries needed to be put in the fry box to make it look full. This was not good for profit or yield (the number of regular serves of cooked fries per kilo of frozen product).

While Gerrie was distracted, a duty manager sneaked a look through Gerrie's work diary, which was normally left unattended in the managers' office during inspections. The mission was to discover the date of the unannounced visit within the next 30 to 90 days. On this occasion we could only work out the days we thought she would not come.

After the dinner rush, Gerrie closed her clipboard and put away her pen. 'Well done everyone. I'll see you tomorrow,' she smiled.

Exhausted and numb, I finished my shift and dragged myself home after thirteen hours at the store. I prayed the next two days of assessment would be incident-free.

Day two was similar to day one but focussed on other areas. The twelve hour of assessment were gruelling and even managers who were rostered off turned up in their uniforms to offer physical and moral support. On day three, Gerrie added up all the scores, wrote detailed comments about unmet standards and completed an extensive 'how to improve' page on each category. As a determined and ambitious general manager I questioned, negotiated and defended the store's position on procedures, store policies and one-off errors. Using a huge calculator Gerrie added up our final scores. Managers and crew who should have left hours earlier hovered nearby awaiting the final tally.

'I told you it would run smoothly.' Gerrie stretched as she

stood up. 'You got an 'A' for Quality, 'B' for Service and an 'A' for Cleanliness. Congrats and well done. It's a terrific result.'

My store manager Bergs wrote the final results on paper and pinned them near the time-clock for all the staff to see. The managers and crew were relieved, proud and exhausted, but I was silent. 'B' for Service was all I heard. I'd expected nothing less than a triple 'A'.

Chapter 8

The Encore

It was 8 am when my pager went off.

Despite our intelligence gathering, thirty-one days after our announced Full Field Gerrie arrived on Mother's Day 1987. We had assumed it wouldn't be that day as we'd spied an entry for a Ronald McDonald performance at another store in her diary. Turns out she'd created a fake entry just in case we tried that trick. Either that, or it's true that not even Ronald works on Mother's Day.

I phoned the Cheltenham store to hear the dreaded words, 'Mich, they're here.'

'Get the new flags out of the manager's office and give them to the maintenance guy to put up now!' An easy score of two points for each flag.

For three months after an announced Full Field I'd refuse all social invitations in preparation for the unannounced visit which would reflect our final score and be an integral part of the franchisees review with McDonald's corporation. My family and friends knew about my quest for triple A's, because I'd previously cancelled engagements at the last minute. Everyone knew not to disturb me or be offended as I would dramatically declare, 'My career and future are on the line'.

My pedantic attention to my pager on social occasions had more than once prompted the question, 'Are you a doctor?'

Once, a consultant didn't arrive within the specified follow-up time and when I queried this he claimed he'd got the dates mixed up. The dates mixed up! The whole store, on a knife-edge from day 31-89, revved up beyond all reason by day 90 and *he* had his dates mixed up? Outrageous! I was furious and my staff resembled a lynch mob.

It was protocol to contact the franchisee when the unannounced visits occurred. Franchisees might be in the middle of family functions or at sporting events but there was an expectation they'd go to the store immediately. One such franchisee, Ross Halliday, was racing in the Clipsal 500 car race when his follow-up occurred. McDonald's frowned on franchisees not being in attendance at their follow-ups and we were never sure if his poor marks were a reflection of his non-attendance.

Ross Halliday and his wife Fiona became good friends of mine. When I first moved to Adelaide to open the Fulham Gardens store in 1992, they often had me over for dinner, even though Ross had originally hoped to get the Fulham Gardens store as it was in his 'patch' or trading area. Ross and I were later on the first South Australian Ronald McDonald Ball Committee together, raising money to build Ronald McDonald House Adelaide. Ross had been the youngest ever franchisee in Australia, and invented the meal deals.

In the years before mobile phones became common, making contact could be difficult, but by the time I had my own store, there was no escaping my duty when my mobile rang loudly at a Davis Cup match in Adelaide, part of our sponsorship of Australian Junior Tennis.

When I arrived at the store my heart was racing as I did a quick evaluation of the mood of the room. Our usual consultant, Gerrie, was seated with a stranger in a suit.

'Mich, I want you to meet your new consultant. He's from Sydney and has just won the Company's prestigious Presidents' Award ...'

I looked at him, suited up, young and handsome apart from his permed hair, like a cool Ronald McDonald. I realised the consultant was still talking.

'... and I thought this was a wonderful chance for him to get to know you and the store.'

Despite the power disparity, over time a rapport would develop between managers, staff members and the consultant. After a number of Full Field assessments, the consultant knew which managers were trying to improve and they were familiar with store goals and focus. I thought having a new person thrust upon the staff at such a tense time was very inconsiderate.

'Get these guys a coffee,' I barked to the front-counter crew. 'I'll be back in a few minutes.'

I sat at my desk staring at the manager and crew rosters. Both needed additional padding. Normally on Sundays I only rostered a Day Manager from 10 am–6 pm and a Close Manager from 4 pm–midnight. Today I needed an extra 12 pm–8 am manager; I called my second assistant as she was very competent.

Now to the crew roster. I drew lines in pencil on the roster for the extra shifts required and listed crew names to match. Then I instructed a crew person who had arrived early for his shift to contact those already rostered on, as well as the extras, to warn them head office had arrived.

But I knew I needed more help so I phoned my BMW-owning friend Simonne, who hadn't worked at the store for three years. While working at Cheltenham she had a history of scoring an 'A' for service, and with our previous 'B' for service, we needed all the help we could get.

'Can you work all day today? It's the Full Field follow-up!'

'On my way.'

The follow-up didn't take as long as the previous visit, and was usually just a single day. It was a review of the previous three-day assessment to ensure standards that were met last visit were still on track and items deemed below standard had been addressed. So I knew extra emphasis would be on service due to our previous score 'B'.

It was the same routine. Twenty timings were done for each lunch, dinner, snack and non-rush snack time. The fastest and slowest times were discarded and the remainder averaged to give an overall score. Timing started as soon as a customer got in a line.

We had conducted two service training sessions since the announced visit. The key points we'd lost last time were for incorrect orders and missing products, with both errors slowing down other service times. The service group had practiced folding size 4, 8 and 12 bags neatly with the M logo facing the customer on presentation. This handover was the opportunity for eye contact and a 'Come back soon' farewell greeting. It wasn't acceptable to present scrunched up bags, or squash too many products into the smaller size 4 bag, or to pass bags to the customer sideways, though it seems these days it is often up to the customer to find their bag and remove it from the counter.

The flat bags had to be fanned to separate them and then stored with the bottom fold section facing upwards for a quick grab and fill system. The bag numbers were an indication of the amount of product to be packed in each bag. A Big Mac wouldn't be placed in a small number 4 bag. Product was not to be packed sideways or upside down. Some current employees might be thinking, 'I didn't know that.'

Since the consultant's first visit, I had run extra back-area meetings highlighting the importance of product availability, speed of product delivery and the overall effect on front counter times. I instructed that the dress bench must be stocked with all products and most importantly, timers kept on the raw produce. It was vital that cheese, lettuce and onions were not left at room temperature for more than two hours.

When I first started at Macca's, lettuce was the most time-consuming ingredient, as they were chopped by hand at the store. It was rumoured that at a horse race several franchisees were discussing the labour intensive job of chopping lettuce with a Victorian lettuce supplier. The supplier suggested pre-cutting and bagging could be done at his warehouse prior to delivery. Problem solved.

The humble tomato arrived in a ten kilogram box at least twice a week. Each tomato was individually placed on a large paper-lined tray with the core pointing down and not touching its neighbours. Maintenance was a daily task and included replacing the paper and discarding any casualties. When needed at the dress bench, the tomatoes were washed, cored and sliced and stacked vertically before a timer was set to one hour and placed on the dress bench. At that time only used in a McFeast, tomatoes were the neediest and most time-consuming raw ingredient

Along with pens, Textas and party-cake knives, the tomato Core-It was a vital piece of McDonald's equipment that frequently went missing. Even when I tied the Core-It to the tomato-slicer table leg with electrical ties it disappeared. The portable tomato slicer also had to be treated with care. The blades were very sharp and had to be cleaned and sanitized after each use. Often a rubber foot/stopper on the leg of the slicer would go missing and the slicer would not sit square. Or a crew person would try to force an oversized or soft tomato through the blades which would get trapped, or worse, push the blades out of alignment. Minor cuts were an infrequent injury at Macca's, though why anyone would try to get trapped tomatoes out of the slicer using their fingers was beyond my comprehension. At any rate the crew knew we couldn't afford to run out of tomatoes during our busy periods as it held up the counter times considerably.

With this in mind, I prayed that all the crew's hard work and training would pay off and that everyone on shift had retained the wisdom of those training meetings. In addition I'd placed printed notes all over the store highlighting Full Field issues. They vied for space with all the usual notes pinned to the walls: ensure you only clock on at your rostered time, wash your hands, use the pay phone not the store phone unless your shift has been altered. On the manager's desk were other reminders: skim tills hourly, conduct travel paths around the block, and toilet checks every 30 minutes.

The 'six steps' were printed and taped to each of the six cash-registers: greet the customer, take the order, suggestive sell, assemble the order, receive payment, ask for repeat business.

There were sample paper cups in all sizes marked with lines demonstrating how far to fill with ice-cubes and a reminder to change the ice-block at the top of the milk dispenser every two hours. I took a moment to check that the orange juice was thawed and dated, and the timers were on the dress bench. These were easy fixes that got zero points at our last visit and nearly cost us the 'A' for quality.

Communication on shift was worth a lot of points and in normal circumstances stores were noisy with managers instructing, cooking timers sounding and a general dining-room buzz. A silent store was not a good sign, but even the best managers and crew could clam up during a Full Field. They wouldn't call out orders or yell to the dining room person to clean up a drink spill in the party room or demand an order go out immediately to a car in the car park. (This only happened when a customer varied a burger recipe and had to wait while we cooked their 'grill order', for example a Big Mac with no pickle). It was frustrating to watch.

A sense of humour *and* a sense of priority were needed during these visits. For excellent front-counter service the confident show-offs who didn't suffer stage fright were rostered on. The kitchen area required calm, orderly staff members and the fry station was best manned by a driven and organised individual. The right people-positioning and product enhanced our chances of a successful day.

There was a good vibe in the store that day and it was noticeable. The managers and crew had made a supreme effort with their appearance; that alone could be worth an extra four to six points. We'd worked on our weaknesses and knew our stuff. And although I was initially unimpressed by the introduction of an extra consultant, it meant I didn't have to follow them around and fill in the score sheets. I was left to run the shift, which was my strength and second-favourite task after cooking fries.

Finally with all the props in excellent working order, damaged mirrors out of the toilets, aces in their places and sliced fresh tomatoes I knew all the rehearsals had been worth it. When the curtain finally came down on this performance we got a standing ovation and a score of BAA.

It took a further two years to earn that coveted AAA. Tony was invited to the Franchisee Convention in Las Vegas in May 1990 and was delighted when we won Outstanding Store Award for 1989 and Bergs won Outstanding Store Manager. Then it was my turn in 1991 to win that award when Bergs was Store Manager of Tony's Southland store and I was again Store Manager of Cheltenham.

Chapter 9

McChelt Chatter

The Cheltenham store had two large gas grills, single platen (flat) with no lid. This was new to me as at my previous stores we only had one grill. The grill man position required the crew member to lay twelve 10:1 meat patties, sear them with a sear tool, turn them with a spatula, season and then pop the reconstituted 10:1 onion on each patty. This was a hero station. 'Sear lay' was the best procedure: as you seared twelve patties you laid another twelve and on it went, constantly moving, turning, searing until you were rostered off the station or told to take a break. It was a true honour to receive the Grill Man Award of a little mounted spatula.

I loved the bun man station, which was the beginning of the burger-making process. Managers would sometimes end up working crew stations to help the team catch up when things got hectic. McHappy day was always a challenge as it was the busiest day of the year for Big Mac orders.

Before the implementation of the clam grill in the 1990s we had a mini clam the size of a jaffle iron. It was perfect for the 4:1 sized patties that we used on Quarter Pounders and McFeasts. We would cook two at a time and always fresh for each order. The mini clams were great for the quiet sales periods. Then when the large clamshell grills came in the grill man position disappeared. We still had a grill man but not an artist on the grill.

When I went to Niddrie McDonald's to learn how to clean the clam, armed with my elbow-long heat-resistant gloves, I was keen to get started and jumped right in.

'My hands are burning!' I yelled only seconds later.

'Have you turned it off?' asked Javier.

Oops. That was a good idea.

While at Cheltenham I often managed the 4 pm to midnight shifts, which meant I also had to watch out for the local troublesome lads when they moved to our store car park after the Southland Shopping Centre closed in the evenings. Whenever I went out to reprimand or negotiate with them, they would salute me and say, 'Attention! Here comes the General!' as my name badge stated GM.

When I first commenced at Cheltenham I was on a travel path and noticed Tony sitting in his car in the Southland car park across the road at 11 pm checking out the store. I snuck up and knocked on his window. After he got over his surprise I assured him he never had to spy on my shifts. He never did so again, at least, not to my knowledge.

Another franchisee quirk Tony had was to call the store at closing time to find out the day's sales. This drove me nuts and I promised my young Store Manager self I would never do that when I became a franchisee. Sometimes you could not shut right on the dot if you were still serving customers, and then parents would be collecting crew. It was the most fraught time of shift management.

Occasionally accidents would slow down our closing

routines considerably. I remember a staff member once slipped while carrying a grill drip tray full of fat to the oil drums outside in the dumpster. The fat and oil splashed all over the walls and ran down the stairs near the back doors. Clean-up that night took an extra two hours. It was disgusting!

One innovative idea that helped with cleaning were the colour-coded cleaning cloths to avoid confusion. Red cloths were used in the dining room and green cloths in the kitchen and behind the counter areas. When I originally trained in dining room service I took three cloths: one for the foil reusable ashtrays, one for chairs and one for the tables. Later mop buckets were also colour-coded red the for dining room and green for the kitchen to match the cloths. Brilliant.

In 1987 Tony charged me with overseeing the building of a world first—a rooftop drive-thru at the Cheltenham store. The only one of its kind at the time, the drive-thru followed the roof line over the existing restaurant to create a second storey. A specially built conveyor brought food from the ground floor kitchen to the second storey booth in under ten seconds, providing faster service for customers. Customers entered the car ramp from Jamieson Street, stopped at the speaker/menu board to give their order, then drove forward to the service window for payment and their food before exiting down the ramp and onto the Nepean Highway. We designed it this way as there wasn't enough room to add a drive-thru on the existing block without losing too much of our already small car park. And the customers clearly liked it—we had a 22 per cent increase in annual sales following the drive-thru's debut.

But it did present many challenges, from the state-of-the-art conveyor machine to the low quality speaker out in the open struggling with all the car park and general neighbourhood noise.

Soon after opening, a crew person stacked a four-cup tray with four large shakes and the weight at the front tipped the tray over and jammed the conveyor, putting a stop to any product reaching the rooftop service booth. An inventive staff member raced over to Southland Shopping Centre and purchased a pink basket and a long rope. A staff member was then sent to the top to haul up the orders before lowering the basket for the next order. I can still see the gobsmacked faces of the McDonald's dignitaries who came to view our award-winning, state-of-the-art drive-thru. They watched for many minutes as orders were pulled up the front counter wall and delivered to the unsuspecting drive-thru customers.

The Breakfast Menu launch in 1989 for some reason is not clear in my mind; perhaps it was those early starts. I know Cheltenham was one of the first restaurants—if not the first—in Victoria to trial the menu. My favourite breakfast item—which no longer exists—was the Big Breakfast with scrambled eggs, a muffin, a piece of sausage meat and a hash brown. I wish they'd bring it back. Before the launch we had hotcake griddles installed to simultaneously cook three hotcakes per serve. It became the most challenging station of all at McDonald's, and weekend breakfasts always saw customers waiting on them. Now they are microwaved.

In 1990 Tony, Bergs and I opened McDonald's first food court store in Australia at the Southland Shopping Centre. New cinemas were being built along with a brand-new food court. We called it the Mini Mac and Bergs became store manager. Even though it was tiny, it was a huge undertaking.

Managing the equipment delivery was an interesting project all on its own, as the supplier delivered equipment for a full-sized store with a drive-thru. Bergs and I sat in the new shop shell for hours that night marking off the list of equipment that had to be returned. Needless to say it was very crowded.

All the other businesses in the food court closed at 6 pm. Soon after we commenced trading, we watched adults wondering where they could purchase a coffee or food to their liking while we fed their kids. So Tony purchased an early model automatic cappuccino machine. It went off! Charlie Bell called Tony 'Mr Cappuccino' from then on. But it was very contentious with Macca's and the other food court cafes. McDonald's Head Office questioned the coffee quality and the local cafes were unhappy about the cheap price.

CHAPTER 10

Hamburger University

The lyrics of Neil Diamond's *They're Coming to America Today* ran through my head as I boarded a January 1989 Continental Airlines flight to Chicago. I was ready to embrace the Windy City; I was off to acquire a degree—yes, a real degree from a registered training organisation—in Hamburgerology that would take two weeks, just a tad faster than my previous degree which stretched to five years.

Hamburger University commenced in 1961 as Ray Kroc's training program, when McDonalds only had 100 stores across America. Ray's goal was to ensure hamburgers bought in Alaska tasted the same as hamburgers bought in Alabama. Hamburger U runs year round, and now trains over 7,500 people each year, making me one of over 80,000 graduates.

Australian McDonald's managers normally travelled to Sydney to complete the ten-day Advanced Operations Course (AOC) as the final step for managers prior to becoming a Store Manager. But I'd been promoted to Store Manager five years earlier without attending an AOC, and so refused to study in Sydney; I needed a serious inducement to sit in a classroom and do another course, especially when I obviously could already do the job.

I knew what one day seminars and conferences were like, and could only imagine how tedious a ten-day version would be. Full of enthusiastic, know-it-all, up-and-coming young things, excited to have two weeks off from the store; people away from home, drinking the minibar dry and running from room to room. McDonald's always insisted attendees share rooms to save money and promote strong friendships. I never looked forward to courses or conventions and avoided them even when I became a franchisee three years later in 1992. I thought of it as boarding school without the nuns but with free alcohol. In fact now there are very few hotels that welcome McDonald's managers en masse. I wonder why?

My boss Tony, a man who thought outside the square, persuaded Sydney Head Office to allow me to complete my training in the US. A fully paid trip to America was the only way he could convince me to attend the training. It was December 1988 and Macca's Australia was preparing to roll out a new breakfast menu. Tony cited this as a reason for me to visit stores in the US to learn firsthand about the breakfast menu. He assured them his store would be the first in Victoria to test the breakfast market. Permission granted. I was to travel early in the new year.

Once clear of customs at Chicago O'Hare International Airport, a limousine whisked me to McDonald's headquarters in Oak Brook, Illinois. I felt like a movie star.

'To The Lodge, young lady?' the limo driver asked.

I learnt that 'The Lodge' was part of the Hamburger University enterprise and was owned by McDonald's, but more importantly, it was run by the Hyatt Hotels Corporation. Fantastic! Just the name, 'The Lodge', conjured up thoughts of

Fred Flintstone or Howard Cunningham in *Happy Days*, going to lodge meetings and trying to become the Grand Poobah. With 250 rooms, The Lodge also catered to the public with actor Bill Murray occasionally booked in to take advantage of the private and secluded surroundings.

After check-in, a staff member gave me a map and explained how to get to Hamburger University via a path alongside a massive lake. She explained that welcome drinks would be held in the hotel bar that evening. So it was off to check out my room, and more importantly to meet my roommate. I mean how bad could it be? I was staying at a Hyatt!

The room was like any four-star hotel room but with the addition of a TV with the Golden Arches showing on the screen, welcoming 'Michele Layet and Lisa Wood'. Of great interest to me was the availability of McDonald's training videos on a dedicated channel; our very own McTV channel! There was no Lisa as yet and as it was still daylight I put on a warm jumper to counteract the bitter January wind, and grabbed my trusty map as I could feel the onset of an adventure. Or at least a long walk to stretch after a long flight.

The lake between The Lodge and Hamburger University (stop laughing) is named 'Lake Fred' after Fred Turner, Ray Kroc's first employee, a former CEO at McDonald's and a life trustee of Ronald McDonald House Charities. The lake was frozen and beautiful, the air crisp as only an American deep winter can produce. All around me there was a calm silence. I sat on a park bench and watched the sun set slowly behind dark winter clouds.

When I returned to my room, Lisa was there. To my relief, we got along straight away. During my stay she was a wonderfully fun roommate and we developed a long-term friendship after our shared Hamburger Uni (HU) experience.

That night I met some memorable people. One woman was an American running the Paris McDonald's on the Champs Elysees. With a French father, my interest was piqued. I silently wondered how you got that gig.

'Hi Michele, nice to meet you. How many staff and managers do you operate?'

'About 120 staff and eight managers,' I replied proudly. Facts and figures, much like the graduated job titles, put stores and managers into a hierarchy. It's like an international language between McDonald's people.

'I have thirty managers, so I have to run two separate weekly managers' meetings,' said Caroline Francoise-Golden. Her response put her at the top of the golden arches pile for our batch of students, regardless of her apt surname. She ran one of the busiest stores in the world. In my mind, and possibly her own, she won the crown to be queen and was the first manager I'd ever met with her own business cards.

Another woman I met was your typical work-hard-party-hard manager of the 1980s. Loud, funny and with bright red-and-purple dyed hair, she was everything I expected of a supervisor of 15 New York stores.

The next morning Lisa and I got up early, ate cream cheese bagels with a touch of caviar in the main restaurant—obviously not a McDonald's—and headed over to the very imposing HU main building. We were welcomed by a professor (yes, that's right, there's a professor of HU), given name badges and directed to our assigned seats in a lecture theatre. There were

230 of us students from Belgium, Canada, France, Holland and obviously the US. I was the lone Australian.

On day one the first order of business at every McDonald's course is the inevitable discussion about rules, regulations, and expectations for the following ten days. We learnt that a couple of students in a previous class stole the HU flag and were sent home immediately. Other rules included no racing or swimming across Lake Fred. It was said that many had tried and failed to complete the swim, standing up knee-deep in the middle of the lake before being sent home for their efforts without graduating. Not much risk of that happening at this time of the year, with the lake often frozen over.

Next we were put into groups and asked to come up with a team name and a rotation plan for the role of group leader. I won the first nomination and was directed to stand on the stage at the front of the lecture theatre.

'G'day,' I channelled my best Aussie bravado into the microphone. 'Our team name is 'Too Hot to Handle' and I'm Michele Layet from Down Under.' So much for staying under the radar. It was 1989 and Crocodile Dundee was well known. Happily the room erupted in applause and I felt welcomed.

Other teams made their presentations as 'In a Pickle', 'The Bad Sesame Seeds' and 'Keen as Mustard'. Over the ensuing days many students would sit around me to hear my Aussie accent; they couldn't get enough of it.

The next group activity was to design a team poster but this became time consuming and I lost interest fast. It had been a long day, and at 30 years of age, I felt too old for this school-kid business. 'I'm done with this,' I announced to the group. 'I'm off to the bar. Who's coming? My shout.'

Day Two was full of lectures on Quality, Service and Cleanliness with a touch of Safety, and Day Three covered Employee Relations which we now know as Human Resources.

That night my team met at the Hyatt bar to strategise and study in preparation for the upcoming Hot Hamburgers competition which promised some light relief after a day learning about pay rates, crew reviews and future US products. Our team was up until 3 am revising topics such as McDonald's history, cooking times and hold-up procedures. The American menu was extensive as they competed with other restaurant's 99c breakfasts, $1.99 lunches and cheap dinners. On the McDonald's American menu were pizza, spaghetti and for breakfast, in-store baked scones. It was impossible for me to learn all the temperatures, times and procedures for these new items/products in one night, so I paid for the drinks and snacks and encouraged my team. I was their mascot and prayed that I wouldn't let them down.

At the end of the course there was an exam, with marks awarded for factual knowledge, contributions to their team (as observed by the Professors), as well as team efforts, ideas, helping others and camaraderie. The student with the highest marks at the end of the ten days would be awarded the Archie, a much sought-after prize. Students with an overall score of 90 and above made the Dean's List. (Yes, there is even a dean at HU.) I was a handicap to my team because questions were specific to America: hiring laws, non-metric weights, odd currency and paper money that was all the same colour. And they had such extensive 'change' rules for the cashiers: emphasising counting back the denominations in a loud clear voice; specifying 'out of …' so that other staff could hear and might remember if there was a customer challenge; the requirement to put large denominations under the till drawer.

On the fourth night we played 'Hot Hamburgers', a beat-the-buzzer style game with extra individual points to our overall exam scores and participation ratings. The electronic score board was enormous and looked as though it belonged in a basketball stadium. The only question I answered correctly was the date of Ray Kroc's death; I remembered receiving an urgent phone call requesting I lower the McDonald's flag to half-mast on the day he died.

On Day Five we toured the Ray Kroc Museum and the Chicago head office. It was great to be out of the lecture theatre after four intense days. With our excited faces pressed against the enormous product-testing kitchen windows at Head Office, we observed chefs trialling fat-free yoghurts, sundaes and shakes—a project McDonald's was working on at the time. Next was Ray Kroc's old office and his barber chair kept in his honour. The Ray Kroc Museum got a giggle out of me because his American accent repeating on a loop-to-loop tape recording brought back memories of listening to my first training tapes some seven years ago.

Everywhere was like a McDonald's version of Disneyland. Ray Kroc and Walt Disney were both born in Illinois, and had met while serving in the same army corps in World War I. Perhaps they'd bonded over shared ideals about the importance of cleanliness and maintaining standards for business success. They certainly both shared an understanding of the importance of providing fun environments for the whole family, and the value of cute life-sized characters to entrance children, and they'd both gone on to develop long-lived and loved companies.

The third Monday in January in the US is a federal holiday commemorating Martin Luther King Jnr's birthday which is actually on 15th January. So after a free weekend there was no class on Day Six! A day off and a city shut down. Nan, an African-American fellow student, invited me to a Martin Luther King Jnr Ball which was to be held in the heart of the City of Chicago. It was exciting to be heading out to an 'Invitation Only' function. So far I'd only been to Planet Hollywood and a couple of nightclubs. A limousine collected us from The Lodge, and on the way, we stopped off to pick up some other friends of Nan's—all McDonald's people—visiting Chicago from various parts of America. We talked over each other, laughed, drank champagne cocktails, and stuck our heads out of the limo sunroof. While I can't remember the name of the warehouse where the function was held, I'll never forget the sight of 500 immaculately dressed African Americans dancing under a giant disco ball in a room full of fairy lights.

Nan was determined to send me home armed with a little more information about life, family and McDonald's through her eyes. I had been upfront in class and pertinent with my many and varied questions, so during the ball she sated my natural curiosity. American managers must hire a percentage of particular ethnic groups to maintain a degree of diversity across the staff. Minimum wage in America is exactly what the phrase describes. In one class Nan had led a vocal discussion about her work in a white neighbourhood and her belief that the local community would benefit if a white manager ran that particular store. Then Jim, a white man, loudly queried his placement in a Harlem store for the same reason. My suggestion that Nan should swap with Jim was well received.

Affirmative action was in full force in the US and another wonderful woman I had befriended during my AOC later told me about her promotion to become a Professor at HU. She was the first black professor at HU and she confided to me that she hoped her promotion was based on ability rather than quotas.

On Day Seven we had the class I was most looking forward to: equipment. I enjoyed the hands-on experience of taking a toaster apart, cleaning and brushing refrigeration condensers and changing exhaust fan V-Belts. McDonald's ran equipment courses up until around 2000, but they no longer exist due to safety issues and the complexity of new equipment. I felt it helped to have an overall idea of equipment problems and possible solutions, for example, knowing to call a plumber for a gas hot-water service and not an electrician.

I was once very embarrassed when a technician arrived to repair the Shake machine and declared, 'The machine isn't plugged in.'

Oops. My red cheeks said it all.

'That'll cost $60 for the call-out and $18 for the first 15 minutes. Have a great day.'

I still regularly clean my home air-con filters and occasionally feel the urge to comb (straighten and clean) the condenser fins on an air-con unit or fridge. My strength prior to the introduction of complicated circuit boards was repairing shake/sundae machines using the Preventative Maintenance Calendar (PMC) cards and equipment manual. The PMC was another vital tool at Macca's; it was an extensive work-in-progress for every store, at every level. Now it is mainly visual checks and calibrations, or noting issues and calling the appropriate technician.

At my own stores I developed the habit of putting screws in a cup (they can disappear) and turning equipment off at the power point before attempting a check-up. From my training I knew to never take a fuse out of a shake machine combo while the power was on, and to always put tape over switches in the office or electrical board whilst changing dining room light bulbs, just in case an enthusiastic manager noticed the lights weren't on … BANG.

The laboratory inside HU was even more impressive than I imagined, with multiple fry vats and Taylor Shake Sundae machines lined up against walls. Six 'professors' in white lab coats greeted our class. The most impressive machine was the shake machine encased in perspex, so that the pumps inside could be seen in action. We commenced with a wide-ranging lesson on soft-drink filters and how to change the many and various cartridges inside it, somewhat similar to our modern-day fridges. I listened to every word Professor Kim Wackerman uttered.

'You have a go, Michele,' he said.

Time to show off. I unscrewed the largest filter of a set of six. Water gushed everywhere.

'Michele, turn the water off first.'

My excitement had got the better of me.

The day continued and I got better at tempering my eagerness. I took a Filet-O-Fish steamer apart and saw the inner workings of a muffin toaster and a hotcake griddle, not yet seen in Australia. It was a valuable day of learning and that night I sorted all my notes after dinner and prepared for a long night of study for the exams the following day.

Maybe it was because of the late night or perhaps I didn't know the answers to many questions, but the exams on Day Eight were a blur. While the marketing, profit, safety and hiring exams were relatively easy (relying on common sense mostly), I struggled with the temperatures and times section. This was not just an American measurements issue—this was to be the bane of my life throughout my Macca's career. Thankfully the tests were multiple choice so I couldn't go too wrong.

I finished later in the day than most, relieved it was all over. I headed to the hotel bar where Ed Renzi, President and Chief Operating Officer US, turned up to wish us the best when we returned to our restaurants, trusting we had learnt valuable lessons. Photos were taken, phone numbers exchanged and I realised, despite my initial hesitation, I had found the course a memorable and uplifting experience.

Exams over, Day Nine was a Question and Answer Panel made up of department heads, corporate staff and the CEO. It was an opportunity for managers to ask pertinent questions about the business. It amazed me that these sessions were used by some managers as an opportunity to denounce their boss, their pay level and or the overall McDonald's system. I must admit I drifted off and only returned to the present when I heard someone say, 'See you at graduation, tonight.'

Knowing it was a popular hobby in the US to collect lapel pins, I'd brought a couple of hundred pins in my suitcase to give away to professors, students and hotel staff. Mine were Australian, state specific and rare. I had promotional burgers, competition pins and some in the shape of Australia. That afternoon students set up pin-boards displaying their wares. Although swapping was encouraged, some purchases occurred at exorbitant prices. I gave mine away freely.

'It's no big deal,' I said refusing the US dollars that were thrust into my hand. 'It's a gift. Please. And thanks for your pin in the shape of the great state of Texas.' I was relieved when all 200 pins were dispensed.

Day Ten was dedicated to the graduation ceremony, and awards were announced in the lecture theatre, with speeches, presentations, and the all important handshake. We enjoyed a lively dinner that night as we exchanged contact details and promised to stay in touch.

In the end I graduated with my Certificate of Hamburgerology but missed out on the Dean's List. Several of my team made the grade which meant possible promotion on return to their restaurants, as well as the all-important pay rise.

Because of my unique situation as one of the first Australians to attend, I didn't receive formal results but a report on my skills was sent back to my Franchisee. Airfares to the US were too expensive in the late 1980s, and most franchisees weren't prepared to spend the money. I was lucky to have my boss Tony support me in this way.

I may not have made the Dean's List but being immersed in this environment gave me a greater understanding about McDonald's and everyday American life than I could ever have imagined.

Chapter 11

Orange Bowl Shenanigans

A very successful-yet-cheap public relations tool for McDonald's is the Orange Bowl, a 45 litre insulated barrel that can be filled with orange syrup, ice and water to make 100 cups of cordial. Originally the cups and syrup were donated for school fetes, kindergarten trivia nights and sporting club fundraisers. While the orange bowls were loaned out with a deposit, sometimes the bowls were never seen again, no matter how much paperwork was filled out to ensure their safe return. False names, phone numbers and addresses were supplied to duty managers so eventually cups and syrup became chargeable. The ice is still free.

The manager's diary had scrawled times of intended pick-ups and drop-offs. Every weekend all the orange bowls would be hauled to the back sink and thoroughly washed and sanitized. With seals as strong as an Esky, you'd pray the lids had been left off to air the bowls during the week so they didn't stink. One hundred cups and a bottle of syrup were placed in each of the bowls. Once readied, the bowls were numbered one to seven and lined up under the front counter.

When a customer arrived to collect their Orange Bowl the Spanish Inquisition commenced:

'Where are the school sports being held? How many will be attending?'

'Can you return the bowl before 6 pm please?'

'We need it back straight after the sports day as it's booked out for tonight.'

'May we have your address?'

'No, we need *your* address because schools shut over the weekend. And your phone number please.'

'Sorry but it's strictly one bowl per event. I can give you extra cups and syrup to refill the bowl.'

'You can return cups and syrup for a refund if they haven't been opened.'

'It's $3 for 100 cups and $3 for a bottle of syrup. The ice is free.'

'You'll get 100 cups of cordial per bowl.'

'We require a cash deposit of $20 for the bowl. It's refunded when you bring it back.'

Bookings could and did go wrong. I learned not to hope for an early return or a fast turnaround for a departure on the same day. Invariably we had to make a quick trip to another store to borrow one during the peak school fete season in Spring.

The extra bookings put pressure on the duty manager but meant more money for the franchisee. In the store safe, a small deposit tin and receipt book resided purely for the orange bowl sales. Every Monday morning an anxious franchisee would hover awaiting the tally and their cash-in-hand bonus. They're running a multi-million dollar enterprise and it's down to the OB money. Sometimes we managers just put the missing dollars in ourselves.

The McDonald's Orange Bowl can still be seen on school

sports ovals, and I know some of you reading this will go to your garage and smile upon your very own Orange Bowl with McDonald's South Oakleigh, Cheltenham or Fulham Gardens written on the outside in bold permanent marker. I too wish I'd kept one for parties at home.

Chapter 12

Ronald McDonald Was Not the Only Clown

Do you remember the Cabbage Patch Kids craze in the mid 1980s? The staff at Cheltenham were not immune, and even brought them into work. I was fascinated by their attachment to these strange dolls so sometimes I hid them around the store and watched as their owners went in search. One day I found the ideal hiding spot. Or so I thought ...

In the middle of a lunch rush, my boss Tony hurried over to tell me an unhappy passer-by had called to complain. The caller's daughter was distraught after noticing a Cabbage Patch Kid dangling from our flag pole. Trying to keep a straight face, I owned up to the stunt and was a little embarrassed as Tony walked away muttering something about 'clowns not setting good examples'. I phoned the caller back to apologise for my thoughtlessness and Sarah, our Community Relations Representative, made a little McDonald's uniform for the daughter's Cabbage Patch Kid. All was forgiven.

You may be wondering how I ever became a franchisee, given my penchant for pranks, but one of my strengths was to face constructive criticism and to learn from my mistakes, as you'll see in later chapters.

To help make it up to them we decided to host a Cabbage Patch Party in the train carriage beside the store for the Cheltenham store's tenth birthday celebration. Over 50 kids and their 'babies' booked out the event in days, and we even featured in the local paper!

Other 'jokers' in the business were a combination of managers, crew and customers. I loved the creative excuses crew members used to get out of work. One crew member called to say he had become ill after drinking an Olympic-flavoured shake. When I called his home to check on his wellbeing his mum was surprised to hear he was unwell, as he'd gone skiing. Another crew person phoned in sick only to fall down a cliff in South Australia on his way to the surf, and became the main news story of the day. My favourite sickie story: while selling merchandise for a friend at the 1993 Big Day Out concert (one of my other jobs while saving up to buy my own McDonald's store, along with merchandise sales at the Australian Open, David Cup and various concerts) I spotted four of my crew heading in my direction. I heard one of them hiss, 'Sh*t, it's Mich!' as they disappeared into the crowd. All bar one had called in sick that day.

Simonne, our overnight manager at Cheltenham, had a circus-master streak along with a strong moral code. We'd recently starting operating 24 hours a day to benefit from Transformers, a nearby nightclub that closed at 2 am. If hungry nightclub patrons wanted to be served, they had to prove they could follow instructions, and so over a number of months Simonne trained our regulars well. As she counted to three they would jump to attention, grinning. We were one of the first stores to open 24 hours, and I reckon Head Office could have benefited from rolling out Simonne's training technique.

One time I remember calling in at 2 am when heading home from a night out, and there was a customer on the staff side of the counter, passed out on the floor. His drunken mates had pushed him over the counter.

Another time two of my best full-time crew girls were caught discretely discussing a marijuana transaction at the front counter—unfortunately they were not in jest. One girl was serving the other while she was on a break, but unbeknownst to them, an off-duty cop was behind her in the queue. As they concluded their deal, he arrested them. I rushed over when I realised what was happening, and begged him to let them finish their shifts before taking them to the station.

'It's Friday night—our busiest time, and they're my best crew. Besides, it was only for personal use.' At least that's what I hoped. They went to court and got off with a stern warning, but I still had to sack them. They'd been great crew members, and on reflection, I would have hired them both again, as they learnt from their very silly mistake.

World famous for its training systems, the McDonald's Station Observation Checklists were not a fail-safe for human error. A lack of detailed training or managers making assumptions about crew knowledge were often to blame for silly errors.

I once asked a crew member to fill up the ice containers under the drink towers at front counter before heading to the safe to get change for the drive-thru register. As I passed through the kitchen I saw him carrying our smallest ice scoop from the industrial-sized ice-maker near the back sink area to the front counter one scoop at a time. At that rate, he would have been there for hours. Bemused, I watched him do this twice and on his third trip I called out, 'Fill up a bucket from the walk-in.'

Another time I heard a crew member shout, 'The coffee machine is flooding!' Water was pouring out of the filter holder and spilling all over the floor. I turned off the power to the unit and pulled out the filter, only to find the entire 12 x 12 cm foil packet sitting in the metal basket, instead of the loose coffee granules. She must have switched off during that training module. It's like leaving the plastic on a cheese slice when you make a toasted sandwich in the jaffle iron! At least the machine didn't need servicing afterwards, as it was just a quick clean-up after that trick.

While not a purposeful stunt, my favourite was observing a keen young trainee water the fake plants in the dining room.

But hands down the best clown I ever met at McDonald's was our security guard, Gary Six Sugars. One night I found him out the back with two tattooed guys, each facing the brick wall with their heads under Gary's burly arms.

'Alcohol isn't allowed in the store, boys,' he said as he squeezed a little tighter. 'Oh, hi Mich.'

'Do you need me to call the police?'

'No. Under control,' he smiled.

I sometimes wondered if customers came to the store to deliberately stir him up. With his unflappable nature, we never had an incident on his watch and I always felt safe with him around. He had a way of keeping things calm— unlike our General Manager doing a surprise night-time visit in his vintage three-piece brown suit. When he demanded two unruly customers stop throwing fries around, it quickly escalated into a food fight involving 50 people. There is an art to controlling fun-loving drunks in the early hours of the morning and he didn't have it. Store managers were used to seeing the concrete lion statues smoking; some local teenagers loved to lodge lit cigarettes in the statues' mouths, back in the days of unrestricted smoking. And of course pickles creatively arranged on the dining room ceiling and windows late on Friday and Saturday nights, was another artistic outlet for our patrons. Our own creative responses ranged from serving food in takeaway bags rather than trays after midnight, leaving pickles off burgers, and having a designated spot outside for customers to leave their alcoholic beverages while they were inside. I'd learnt the hard way not to take booze off customers.

Our official clown, Ronald McDonald, was created and portrayed by Willard Scott, a well-known American weather man. In one of the first TV ads in 1963, the 'hamburger-happy clown' had a paper box on his head and a paper cup as his nose, and later he was sitting on a pitched roof with a foam Filet-O-Fish box as a hat, armed with a fishing rod. Australia's first Ronald was Bartholomew John, who starred as Dr Chris Piper in the Australian TV soap opera, *The Young Doctors*.

At times Ronald McDonald was said to be one of the most recognisable characters in the world, second only to Santa or Mickey Mouse. You will never see two Ronald's at any one time. There is only one per state ensuring young children's total belief in this character. He never, ever, advertised or sold product. Instead he helped children learn to cross the road and taught them what to do in case of fire. His associate, the

Hamburglar, was never allowed inside the restaurants when Ronald was visiting, because he was the naughty one who steals your food.

When working in South Australia, I remember the state Head office advertised for a new Ronald McDonald, and a woman applied. She was unsuccessful, unfortunately. Apparently they had a more suitable applicant, with previous clown experience, skills in balloon blowing and magic tricks, who was willing to travel all over the state. There was an audition process, and they had to pass police checks. I always wonder what she would have been like, though. Can you imagine a female Santa?

Ronald—or Ronnie, as employees affectionately call him—is a one-man band. He truly is magical and can do balloon tricks that we mere mortals can only dream of. When Ronald was invited to stores for fundraisers, McHappy Days, store openings and store anniversaries, the staff—including me—would get very excited. At the 2000 Sydney Olympics, Simonne and I met the flesh-and-blood Ronald quite by chance and had our photo taken with him and our Australian flag. It was one of my best days ever.

I've seen children's faces light up when Ronnie visits Ronald McDonald House. They race to the playground to hug and talk to him. At the Melbourne Royal Children's Hospital McDonald's store, the giant fibreglass Ronald-on-a-park-bench in the dining room actually spoke to children when they sat down next to him.

When my fibreglass Ronald-on-a-park-bench at Fulham Gardens was torched, the staff respectfully covered him with black plastic bags. They didn't want the children to see him in that state—or perhaps it was for my benefit as I was more likely to burst into tears than the children. A new Ronald-on-a-park-bench cost $8000, and I just couldn't afford it at the time. His big red feet were all that survived. I still have them on display in a glass cabinet at home.

One thing I never got to do during my twenty-six years was attend an International Ronald McDonald Clown Convention. I'm told more than 500 clowns convened for their annual get-together. I've always wondered if they went in costume.

In case you can't tell by now, I love all things Ronald McDonald. His big boots, his red hair, his huge smile, and of course, his merchandise: dolls, books, t-shirts and watches, videos and the Little Golden Book, *Ronald McDonald and the Tale of the Talking Plant*—I have them all.

Finally, what happened to all the other characters, I hear you ask? I wish I knew. It's years since I've seen Big Mac the policeman, the Fry Kids, or the Hamburglar. Grimace is still around as the purple blimp, Birdie the Early Bird was very popular years ago, but where has Mayor McCheese disappeared to? He was not re-elected Mayor of McDonaldland, obviously.

Chapter 13

Fundraising and McLala Day

Fundraising for the Ronald McDonald House Charities (RMHC) is at the heart of each and every Macca's store, yet we've always played the charity down. This may sound like company speak but it isn't. I've seen tough men and women cry, laugh, celebrate and collapse in grief around children with cancer. To visit a house, or be involved in supporting one, is a privilege.

The Ronald McDonald House Charities began in 1974 in America, when football hero Fred Hill had to sleep in the hallway outside his sick daughter's hospital room while she underwent treatment for leukaemia. Seeing other parents in the same predicament, he drummed up support to buy a large home near the hospital; a place where parents could rest and still be close to their sick children. Together with his football mates, the staff at The Children's Hospital of Philadelphia, and local McDonald's restaurant owners, they raised money to purchase and renovate a large house close by the hospital, to provide accommodation to families with sick children. The first Australian Ronald McDonald House opened in Sydney in 1981, with the second opening in Parkville Melbourne in 1986. There are now 16 houses across Australia.

Every year stores Australia-wide raise money for Ronald McDonald Houses. They run raffles, car washes and chocolate drives, and create themed baskets of goodies made up of local donations to sell via silent auctions at the annual state balls. Sausage sizzles, bicycle rides, trivia nights; you name it, a McDonald's store somewhere has done it. Every cent raised at these events goes directly to the Ronald McDonald Charities programs to benefit the children. All the running expenses for the houses, such as admin, staff and management costs, are borne by the company. Cleaning bees were organized at the Houses in the 1980s and staff got an opportunity to see the benefit of their fundraising. The volunteering day would finish with a barbecue and a visit by Ronald McDonald himself. We were always mindful to not disturb the families living in the house at the time.

At Cheltenham in the spring of 1984—just after the Los Angeles Olympics—we ran a seven kilometre wheelbarrow race from the store to the Cheltenham Town Hall to raise money to establish Ronald McDonald House Parkville. Our goal was to raise $1,000. Two teams competed by pushing a wheelbarrow with a child or small adult along the course, with team members sponsored for the kilometres we ran. The young guns at the store wanted to compete against an Olympian, and fortunately for me, I happened to know one. I brought in the big guns for my team with my brother Paul, a very good distance runner, and his mate Michael Hillardt, an Australian middle distance runner who reached the 1500m semi finals of the Olympics just a few weeks earlier. Geoff Morley and a lovely team of Cheltenham crew led the opposing team. It was gruelling but my competitive streak shone through again.

Running alongside Paul and Michael—who led the race the entire seven kilometres pushing a wheelbarrow each—I made it to the Town Hall but couldn't face the return trip even though I hadn't pushed the wheelbarrows an inch. (Our passengers, tiny crew member Sharon Spragg and Sarah's 8-year-old daughter 'Shorty', were very light, but they were still too heavy for my dodgy back. Poor Shorty still has a fear of wheelbarrows!) Police friends who were monitoring the race along the highway again came to my rescue, and a few of us received a ride back to the store in their divvy van. We raised just over $1,000 for Ronald McDonald House and got our photo in the Macca's magazine. And Michael Hillardt is still a close family friend.

The annual state balls were events not to be missed and important revenue raisers for the Ronald McDonald Houses. Early balls had 300 attendees but now 1,000 people attend them, and they are booked out well in advance. I used to take my store managers, friends and my mum. The managers loved the lead-up to the big night; hairdos, nails, fake tans and new frocks. The night always delivered.

When I was General Manager of Cheltenham in 1986 I was honoured to be invited to join the Victorian RMHC Ball Committee, as usually only franchisees are involved. Later in South Australia I was the Chair of the South Australian Ball Committee. As a franchisee and member of the RMHC Ball Committee I would ensure the silent auctions didn't go too cheaply. Over the years I was the successful bidder on a number of items including a cellar of wine and a trip to see the set of TV show *McLeod's Daughters*. While my best silent auction result was the year I successfully bid on a red Jeep, my favourite silent auction memory was in the late 1990s in South Australia when I won an inflatable raft full of fishing gear. At 1 am as the night was drawing to a close, I could hear Mum ask a friend to bring the car round and take me home immediately. I was sitting in the boat, pulling on the oars, and singing *Row, Row, Row Your Boat* at the top of my lungs. When I got home I put it straight into my swimming pool!

South Australia's first Ronald McDonald House in Adelaide required $1.2 million to build, and I was proud to be involved in raising those funds and representing South Australia's franchisees on the board of Ronald McDonald House Adelaide when it opened in March 2000. I stayed on the board throughout my years in South Australia, and served on committees for Balaklava Race Days, Crew Rallies and of course, the RMH Adelaide Ball.

Another way we liked to support the local community was special events. In 1990 we helped the local community celebrate Senior Citizens Week by hosting afternoon tea in our Red Rattler train carriage at Cheltenham. We invited a different Senior Citizen Club for each day of the week, and played Bingo after the meal. And in 2001 I held a special fundraising day to support Centacare in their provision of respite accommodation for children with autism. Inspired by Mario Corena, a local father who'd beaten two bouts of cancer and was volunteering for Centacare, we created McCorena Day, and raised $800 by giving away 800 Happy Meals in exchange for a $1 donation each

The first McHappy Day in Australia was held in 1991, with a percentage of every Big Mac sold going to the Ronald McDonald House Charities. Celebrities (or famous people as they were known in my time) offered their time to attract and serve customers. The yearly event takes place in 36 countries worldwide and funds sixteen properties in Australia alone.

My first McHappy day as a franchisee was a huge success. While all our special guests were hardworking and generous with their time over the years, none of them had the magnetism of the iconic lead character of the *Humphrey B Bear Show*, who agreed to work a McHappy Day shift for my Fulham Gardens store in 1993. Families arrived early to organise tables and there was a buzz of excitement in the air; the front counter a sea of faces. Humphrey sneaked in via the staff entrance and as the crowds spotted him a deafening cheer erupted. Parents lifted children onto their shoulders for a better view. While some children cried with joy most just waved happily hoping to be noticed. While he shook paws with fans his minder handed out autographed picture cards. (I still treasure mine.) He blew his signature air-kisses, performed his cumbersome dance but never ventured past the front counter, just in case he was mobbed.

Besides the excitement for the littlies, the joy with Humphrey was that parents actually spent money and purchased Big Macs. When teen idols visited, teenagers turned up to meet them, screamed, occasionally cried but then often left without spending a cent.

In May 2002 Fulham Gardens came third in South Australia for most Big Macs sold on McHappy Day—824 in one day. By drawing upon our extensive range of contacts in the community we were able to program a full day of entertainment and activities for our customers, including appearances by popular radio DJs, TV weather presenters and sports reporters, sports stars and our local firefighters. That year we even managed a live cross on SAFM and news coverage on Channel 7.

State marketing managers matched stores to celebrities based on convenience for the celebrity, store location and demographics. My Fulham Gardens store was near the airport which meant it was convenient to anyone who flew in. Over the years I hosted TV game show host Tony Barber at the Cheltenham store, journalist and *A Current Affairs* host Michael Schildberger and radio broadcaster Amanda Blair. I have pictures of federal politician Amanda Vanstone wrapping Big Macs behind the counter. Watching customers faces when they realised someone famous was serving them at the drive-thru was priceless. During my 16 year tenure as a franchisee, Humphrey B Bear proved the biggest drawcard in terms of customer numbers and Big Macs sold, eclipsing even the very popular cast of *McLeod's Daughters*. It was amazing that a big bear with a chequered vest and no pants could have so much power!

Chapter 14

The Board, the Watch and the Ten Year Ring

Franchisees were usually selected from within the company, after an average of twenty years working their way up through the system as crew, managers, or consultants. Others were hired from outside, but these were usually businessmen with experience and money. I was never a crew person and so it was highly unusual for me to be standing in front of the McDonald's board members early in 1992 to determine my suitability as a franchisee. It was just ten years since I first secured that trainee manager position at South Oakleigh.

After eight years running Tony's stores and winning the Outstanding Store Manager award, I'd gone as far as I could as a franchisee's employee. Knowing I was ambitious and hard-working, the company asked me if I would like to become a training manager for Victoria. While I was flattered, I told them I'd rather work for myself and be my own boss, which led to this interview when opportunities arose in Perth and Adelaide.

I'd dressed with care that morning, wearing my one-and-only freshly dry-cleaned navy suit, new shoes and pill-free pantyhose. As a subtle attempt at showing my credentials I'd also chosen to wear my Ronald McDonald watch which I'd won at a leadership course, my Ronald McDonald House committee-member pin, and my McDonald's pinkie ring, which I'd recently been awarded for ten years of service.

Also there to support me were two company sponsors Tat Cork and Julie Owen, senior executives who had nominated me as a potential franchisee. I sat in front of the committee in between Tat and Julie, mentally reminding myself to breathe. *Is this what I really want? Do I really want to move to Adelaide or Perth? What if I go broke?* Unhelpful doubts rushed through my mind.

If successful, I would leave an annual salary of $85,000 plus car and profit sharing on a sliding scale for sales in excess of $5 million per annum, to open up a brand new store with uncertain sales projections, in a state still struggling to beat Hungry Jacks. I'd also had to leave my family and friends. If all went well in my first year of operation, I would earn between $30,000 and $50,000. The driving force was to become my own boss, eventually own multiple high-volume stores, and make lots of money. As I used to tell my brothers when I was 15 years old, 'I want to be filthy stinking rich.'

In the three short months since I lodged my application, my franchisee Tony at Cheltenham had helped me rehearse succinct answers to questions that were likely to be thrown at me. As protocol required that I be unaware of which board members would attend, I didn't know who would be throwing the questions.

For the next hour I was grilled about my experience, business acumen, suitability and adaptability.

'How will you cope living away from friends and family?'

'What if you lose your investment?'

'What can you offer the business that is different to other franchisees?'

I'd been told prior to the interview that the person who knew me the least would ask most of the questions and that turned out to be the Chief of Finance. What a grilling—no wonder the young guy before me struggled with the profit and loss questions. (He was not selected that day but went on to become a successful franchisee in later years.)

Taking my time to answer questions carefully was my plan, and I consciously slowed down my usually rapid rate of speech. Then out of the blue came a question no-one had prepared me for.

'As a franchisee how would you have handled the union situation at Cheltenham?' This was to test my loyalty toward my direct supervisor whose lack of resolution of ongoing crew members complaints about frequent unplanned overtime, a lazy shift manager and lack of promotions meant Cheltenham became the first store in McDonald's Victorian history to have a staff member form a union. In fact one of my sponsors and I had met through this circumstance. My reply—that I would implement and adhere to the union's suggestions—was met with approval.

During the interview Charlie Bell, then on the board of McDonald's Australia, stuck his head in and apologised for not attending the interview, as my application had his blessing. The interview concluded soon after. Determined to have the last word, as I shook everyone's hand, I thanked them for the opportunity and promised to never let them down and to make them proud. I'm pleased to say it was a promise I kept.

Relieved the interview was over, I expected it would be days before a decision was made. But while having coffee with Charlie downstairs, my sponsor came in to congratulate me.

That day in 1992 I was the very first female franchisee to come through the ranks. And even though accepting the offer meant I lost out on the long service leave I would have received had I stayed on at Cheltenham for an extra two months, Tony's thoughtful parting gift of my company car more than made up for it. Now at least I had something to drive to my new home.

After the offer to become a franchisee came the decision as to which store. I was offered a choice of locations in Perth or Adelaide. Adelaide was more tempting to me for a number of reasons. It was closer to Melbourne, and I had close friends and my godchild living there. The Fulham Gardens store was available as the franchisee-in-training, Tony Cataudo the Tomato Guy, had changed his mind at the last minute. He decided to keep running his business which supplied all McDonald's stores in the state with their fresh produce: lettuce, tomatoes, onions, etc. Later on his daughters worked for me, as well as his niece. They were a great hardworking family, and he is still supplying Macca's today

Chapter 15

My Own Golden Arches

The alarm sounded at 3 am. It was time to pack the Honda Accord with my suitcase, a new computer and a three-in-one stereo; a goodbye gift from my Cheltenham store managers which I still can't throw out to this day.

I'd refused all offers of farewell gatherings as I preferred to grab quick individual goodbyes without tears. But looking back at my cats Monti and Louis in my bedroom window as they watched me leave really hit home, and I cried hard. They wouldn't join me until I had rented my own place in Adelaide.

With mixed emotions I headed for the South Australian border. I knew the route well, having made the trip several times over the past six months in preparation for the December 1992 opening. I strictly observed speed limits on entering and exiting towns after a previous hefty fine and loss of demerit points. I had been trying to save money by driving but after that run-in with Highway Patrol decided it was cheaper to fly with the budget airline Compass. It was a time of uncertainty as I wasn't yet earning any income but still had to pay salaries to my two new managers-in-training.

I'd arranged accommodation with good friends, who were the parents of my two-year-old godchild. They were the main reason I accepted a store in South Australia rather than Western Australia, and their son Jack Batty later came to work for me in his teens, before trying his hand at state politics.

Once I'd emptied the car at their house I drove to the site of my new store. Its wooden frame sat proudly on the asphalt pad of the Fulham Gardens' shopping precinct. I visited daily as the building progressed and held a small celebration when Ronald McDonald, seated on a park bench, was installed. It was an exciting time.

Opening a new store meant a range of tasks needed to be performed in logical order. McDonald's Head Office assigned a consultant to first-time franchisees to assist them to navigate the huge workload quickly and efficiently. The first task was hiring a crew and getting them trained, in a state that I knew very little about, geographically speaking. The local Commonwealth Employment Service (CES, a government employment organisation) were very supportive and offered me their facilities to interview and hire crew members. Keen to encourage youth employment in their area, the staff quickly screened applicants before booking suitable candidates in for a final interview with me or another McDonald's representative. It was an arduous task. The process required a multitude of application forms, induction briefings and second interviews. Managers from other stores offered to help me, and a couple of franchisees also donated their time. (You may think it unusual to help someone who is soon to be a competitor, but the informal support system was one of the great strengths of McDonald's, and most franchisees abide by it. I went on to train many new franchisees, and most of them are still in the system. It's just what we do. But the owner of the store nearest to me did not help at all.)

As we were sorting through the mass of screened applicants and placing them into 'interview' and 'reject' piles, I remember my consultant Raff taking an application I'd just put in the 'interview' pile and placing it in the 'reject' pile.

'Put it back,' I said, annoyed.

'She's too old,' replied Raff. The applicant was only 17.

'But I'll need casual managers at some stage.'

'Still … too expensive.'

Sarah's credentials were exceptional: long term member of the Australian Girls' Choir, available to work anytime, and she owned her own car. I won out that day, and Sarah turned out to be one of my best hires ever. She went on to win every prestigious McDonald's management award, became the Fulham Gardens store manager and eventually the McDonald's crew training coordinator for South Australia.

Raff was a great consultant and is now a franchisee himself. His wife worked with me at Fulham Gardens for a few years—all part of the big McDonald's family.

After a gruelling two nights of interviews, we'd sorted over 200 applications and hired 70 people. With relief, I called and congratulated all the successful applicants and invited them to their first crew orientation meeting at the CES offices. The whole process was completed in just two weeks. Unsuccessful applicants were contacted by my trainee managers with a promise to keep their application on file should a position became available. Some did eventually come to work at Fulham Gardens when original hires didn't start or couldn't handle the training.

At the paid orientation meeting the fledgling crew members met the management team, were fitted with uniforms, given a tax declaration form to complete and a signed copy of the McDonald's Staff Rules and Regulations form to take home for light reading. Commonwealth Bank of Australia tellers also attended the orientation and organised staff bank accounts, which was a huge load off my payroll shoulders. Sometimes, if it was a newcomer's first job they might forget to give me bank details. They'd call and ask why their pay hadn't gone through and I'd have to write a cheque or put it through the following week. It was very important to them to get that first pay.

The last item on the orientation agenda was the importance of the training roster which the managers explained in detail with each crew person individually so that they were prepared for the various stores and new people they would meet.

Prior to the crew orientation meeting, I ordered uniforms from Joseph Dahdah Apparel and contacted five Adelaide stores to assist in training my 70 new staff. My nearest neighbour declined because he saw me as competition. I understood; the greatest threat to the sales of a McDonald's store is the opening of another store in the area.

I then met with the four local franchisees, store managers and rostering managers who had offered to train my guys. Although I supplied time cards for my staff, only the one franchisee sent me an account for the training he'd provided. The staff was divided into four groups to commence training: front-counter, grill, drive-thru and closes. Drive-thru trainees headed to Darlington and Camden stores, while the rest went to the city stores and a shopping centre food court where they knew a lot about prompt service and dining room cleanliness.

Close shifts are wash-up, grill-close and front-counter. Cross training would be done later when Fulham Gardens opened.

The full-time maintenance guy I'd hired in the first week quit before starting so one of the unsuccessful original applicants was hired to begin immediately. New staff with no previous training had to deal with travelling long distances from home, followed by parking woes at city stores. It was a massive operation.

I hired an experienced Assistant Manager from Newcastle with glowing references to do the dinner and night shifts and I managed the breakfast and lunch shifts until our trainee managers were competent. The trainees had to complete the Basic Operations Course before they were allowed to run shifts unsupervised. I was lucky to get a fully trained shift manager in 1993. A new store at West Terrace was not opening for a few months so Kerry Wright was available to work with me. Her franchisee Peter wanted her trained on the latest equipment and in the new roster, payroll, end of month and ordering systems—all of which I had—and in return I received a wonderful shift manager at no charge. Kerry went on to the US and became a Professor at Hamburger University. She's still a great mate to this day.

I chose not to hire managers from existing stores despite the many applications I received when the advertisement hit the newspaper. While it would have been a cheaper and faster way to acquire managers, that approach often brought long-term issues. Older staff wanting to move sideways often had ingrained habits, plus I didn't want to cause anxiety amongst my South Australian franchise peers with whom I was not yet fully acquainted.

It was stressful paying three managers salaries and the costs of crew training while I wasn't earning an income. I had only started this adventure with $30,000 in the bank, and costs were adding up. I also needed to factor in acquiring my own accommodation.

When I came back to Melbourne after hiring my crew, Mum helped me enter new employees' details into the computer and set up an old-school filing system, complete with a grey three-drawer cabinet. She painstakingly wrote the names of my 70 new employees on manila foolscap files and ordered them alphabetically. I still have some of them today, with her distinctive handwriting. I was the first franchisee in South Australia to process my staff's pay internally via computer. Other stores were still using the Simplex time clock method with bookkeepers to process their staff's pay and prepare monthly accounts, profit and loss statements and group certificates manually, with all the attendant bookkeeping fees that entailed.

This was just another in a long line of firsts for me and South Australia that year: I was the first female franchisee in the state, the first to install self-filtering fry vats, and the first to install the combo shake/sundae Heat Treat machine which pasteurised itself and only needed cleaning weekly instead of nightly. At a cost of $25,000, the saving in labour to clean the machine was a crucial selling point. Unfortunately the predicted savings weren't evident in my first year due to constant breakdowns, and eventually I had to replace it after protracted negotiations with the supplier. I'd come a long way since that five-headed spindle in 1982.

There wasn't much opportunity to have input in the

equipment package or dining room décor, as these had been ordered months in advance by the previous franchisee-in-training who had decided not to proceed with owning the store. I ordered and paid for operating supplies, food, paper, promotional items and uniforms with my consultant breathing encouragingly down my neck. If he'd had his way I would have gone into overdraft immediately. I had to keep reminding him whose money it was.

Operating supplies are along the lines of household items: ice scoops, spatulas, mops, buckets, rubbish bins, baskets and rubber gloves. Everything was brand new; it was exciting. There was even a sparkling brand-new Canon calculator for the office. For me, accustomed to second-hand cast-offs from someone else's school days, this was a big deal. There were no biro scribbles ... yet. That would come later.

To ease some of the financial burdens I signed on to what's termed a Before Full License contract. Under this arrangement, the Corporation paid the lease costs for the building, main equipment, décor and dining room. Then, within three years but not before thirteen months, I was expected to purchase the store outright from the Corporation. This allowed me to get on with running the business and grow sales rather than concern myself with the availability of money to pay down an overdraft.

When the time came for me to borrow $700,000 to buy my small store, some 18 months later, my application was denied by the Commonwealth Bank of Australia. This was the first time the CBA had declined to lend money to a McDonald's franchisee for a store in South Australia— this was one first I didn't want to be part of. It had never occurred to me they would say no. Other franchisees I spoke to questioned the Bank Manager's decision, especially his response was that my sales projections of $1.5 million per annum were not realistic. Maybe, but my colleagues believed the loan was refused because I was a single woman. I went straight to Westpac with the same projections and was welcomed with open arms. That now made three McDonald's franchisees banking with Westpac. The CBA stranglehold was diminishing. And when I sold the business in 2003 annual sales had grown to $3 million.

I had been selected from the field of franchisee applicants because of my strong operations skills and I was put to the test many times when I had to extend my personal budget to run the store at an AAA rating standard. Franchisees paid for all equipment repairs, insurance, electricity, accountants, phones etc. and after warranties expired, repairs bills began to rise.

McDonald's marketing structure is similar to Australia's political arrangement of local, state and federal governments. There was often discussion about relinquishing power to one or two bodies. I contributed financially to three budgets: the National Marketing budget, which all stores in the country contribute to, the State Marketing budget, and the Local Store Marketing (LSM) budget, which allows individual store franchisees to make their own decisions re dollars spent.

My marketing consultant Robyn was enthusiastic as this was her first McDonald's store opening. I needed to constantly remind her of my budget. Strangely the state and federal McDonald's budgets don't set aside an allowance for these costs. I vigorously debated the expense of a Ronald show, letterbox drops and full-page spreads in the local paper with her. We discussed opening month discounts, but decided against it so as not to antagonise my neighbouring franchisees. I thought curiosity and awareness of the construction site would entice the locals to try us out but I heard this was not always the case. It took me a while to learn that Hungry Jack's ruled the South Australian fast food market, and we had a fierce competitor only one kilometre down the road.

To counter opposition from local residents I thought carefully about opening hours. Although my actual store location was not in a residential zone there were many houses nearby and across the street. I was mindful of resident's concerns but keen to harness the late night trading of Hungry Jacks. There was a large loan to repay, after all. Our hours of operation in the end were 6 am to 2 am on Friday and Saturdays and normal business hours for the rest of the week.

While the original store design didn't include a playground or a patio, I knew it was vital to have a playground from my experiences at Cheltenham. I pleaded my case with the Corporation, stressing that it was crucial given the demographics of the area to build sales and birthday party revenue in the future. Why wait to build it later and disturb operations? I even offered to pay for it myself and as McDonald's knew exactly the state of my bank account they made it happen without my financial input. My dream of having the first McMaze playground in South Australia would be the icing on the celebration cake, which I invited the local Mayor to come and cut on opening day. That playground went on to become an integral part of the Fulham Gardens store for parties, fundraising and improved street presence.

In another Fulham Gardens building 'first', I decided to clad the building in Colorbond instead of the more popular bricks favoured in South Australia. Colorbond was easy to construct and even easier to build with, and cheaper to maintain, as any damaged wall panels could be quickly replaced. In fact, they were only defaced once during my twelve years at Fulham Gardens, when the Adelaide Football Club (Crows) won the AFL Grand Final against St Kilda in 1997. That first premiership was a big deal for us as the Crows Football Club was quite close by. A few years later Charlie Bell offered to brick it over at the company's cost but I declined because by then the locals had affectionately named it 'The Shed'.

As I had given up smoking in 1991, I made the momentous decision to make the store the first smoke-free McDonald's restaurant in Australia. Prior to leaving Cheltenham, I had banned smoking in the office, crew room and manager's area to encourage others to quit, and I must admit, make it easier for me to stay on course. The benefits were obvious, but we operated, like most businesses at that time, with half the dining room designated a smoke-free zone. The Victorian Government didn't catch up to South Australia in banning smoking in dining rooms until 2001. In the intervening years I recall visiting friends in Melbourne and being surprised at them lighting up inside.

While we didn't allow customers to smoke inside, it was still legal for them to smoke in outside dining areas—even if they were right next door to playgrounds. So during construction we installed two fixed ashtrays outside in the patio area but after twenty complaints from non-smoking parents soon after opening, I decided to ban it there too. For some time the staff had to chastise customers for smoking inside the restaurant and were often abused for their trouble. These were the fraught, early days of the progression to non-smoking restaurants when frazzled customers were not the least bit interested in our concerns for their health, impressionable young children, or the regulations.

Another 'first' during store setup was the agreement I won with State Head Office that Fulham Gardens would not serve salads. This was a great saving for me in both labour and food costs. Looking back, this was unusual as South Australian stores were trialling salads ahead of their Australian rollout, though they were not selling well. It took more than a decade for customers to embrace that particular product Australia-wide.

The most difficult task was to select a realistic opening date, one that balanced my need to open quickly so I could start recouping some of my investment while allowing enough time to finish construction and fit-out. With my dollars rapidly depleting, Saturday 5th December 1992 was chosen for our grand opening. A full-page ad in the local *Weekly Times Messenger* newspaper meant the commitment had to be met. We offered free Cheeseburgers with the purchase of another burger, and Ronald McDonald, the Hamburglar and a face painter would be present throughout the day. I planned to hang balloons and streamers from the rafters and make the day as enjoyable as possible for our youngest customers. I received favourable press the week before as well, with a long article about the local employment opportunities I was providing to young people in the area, as all of my new employees were aged between 14 and 21. The *Weekly Times Messenger* also reported on my desire to foster ongoing involvement with the local community through supporting local schools, sporting groups such as Junior Tennis Australia, Clean Up Australia, Ronald McDonald Houses and the Australia Day Council Aussie of the Month program. Handover from the builders loomed and overlapped with my need to get inside the store and set up. External and internal menu-boards required pricing, floors needed to be scrubbed, stainless steel polished and operating supplies unpacked and stored. Then there was the rather important task of scheduling the food and packaging deliveries.

A major job prior to opening a new store is cleaning after the builders have left. Full-time employees, already on the payroll, were on bended knees with scrubbing brushes in hand. Floor tiles needed to be scoured several times. Technically, until the builders hand over the keys no one is allowed inside but with our time constraints and the late decisions on the playground and patio, we couldn't wait. With cooperation, everyone worked side-by-side, next to and around each other. It was like a giant twister board.

We started with the stockroom and then moved on to the manager's office. My computer guy from Victoria had commandeered the tiny space which also housed the electrical boards and switches. The cash register guy I had flown in from Sydney was hovering as were the local technicians from Taylor Company, there to install and train my staff on the Combo Heat Treatment unit, self-filtering vats and grill maintenance.

Despite the building, plumbing, aircon and electrical systems all being completed, there was a mountain of questions that required on-the-spot answers from me. Like a whirling dervish, I tackled all questions.

'When can I install the dining room mirrors?'
'Mich, the guy's here to put up the fridge curtains!'
'Hey Love, where can I drop off these sixty chairs?'

With the opening day timer counting down, the chaos continued.

'Dining room tables have arrived.'
'We're missing a chair from this one'
'Where are we putting this pile of plastic?' Tempting as it was to scream, 'Anywhere!', I knew I had to carefully consider the placement of toilet roll holders, mirrors and even the time clock if everything was to be right.

The fire-extinguisher installation proceeded without problems but there were endless discussions about my choice of positioning for the ice and washing machines. I walked away from that conversation. There was no peace to be found anywhere. (My favourite meditation place, the fry station, wasn't operating yet.)

Basic Operations Course BOC 1983

McDrive-Thru

The Big McBlaze

Ronald McDonald fleeing to safety. Carolyn Chataway, Sharon Spragg and me

My McBoss, Tony Wither

Sarah Cain with Cabbage Patch Kids McDonald's uniform

Back in the day

McHappy Day Yvette Smith, Tony Barber and me

Wheelbarrow race 1984

Ronald McDonald and Mike Hillardt

Shanghai McNugget promotion 1987

Sarah Cain and Bergs Goodluck standing on the new McDrive-Thru

Oustanding Store Award 1989

McHappy Day with Humphrey B Bear 1993

McHappy Day. Me with Amanda Blair

Chapter 16

The Grand Opening

Six people were already lined up out the front when I approached the store on launch day December 5th 1992. A feature of our advertising was that the first five customers would each win fifty-two free breakfasts for the year. The 260 free meals were an easy way to increase publicity AND reward loyal customers. The adrenalin was pumping and I prayed the day would be a success and that finally some money would be banked. Sales of at least $21,000 per week were needed to cover salaries and creditors. The beauty of McDonald's is that cash flow is instant as no one ever owes us money.

That first morning as I entered the back door at 5 am I was greeted by the panicked voice of my shift manager David.

'The registers are offline!'

My heart sank. Not a good start.

'It'll be okay. Just call the help desk.'

With a smile plastered on my face, I went to my new front door and presented the five breakfast vouchers thinking, *Only 255 free meals to go.* But I learnt the hard way that we hadn't been specific enough in our advertising. The voucher hadn't stated one meal per person per week, just 52 free breakfasts. One winner bought in ten of his family the next day and followed up the next weekend with the same numbers on Saturday and Sunday—very cheeky. As a franchisee I decided not to go on counter that first day because I begrudged every single voucher and giveaway. It was my money.

This sentiment didn't always bode well. Once, I didn't allow a customer to order orange juice instead of coffee with their meal deal because the OJ was more expensive. They walked out without purchasing anything. Aghast, I felt compelled to run after them and apologise before I ordered them a free meal with OJ. They went on to eat breakfast at my store every Monday to Friday until the day I sold the store. What price can you put on loyalty? McDonald's marketing policies eventually caught up and patrons could request any drink with a meal.

The first day the store was full of casual visitors who annoyed me. I didn't want to chat with other franchisees, sticky-beaks or head office staff. I was aware of my rudeness by not meeting and greeting but, in fact, opening days are stressful and require full concentration. I wanted to work with my managers and crew, not meet and greet the hoi-polloi. Was it too much to expect to be able to look after paying customers, iron out equipment problems and engage with my staff, or even to go to my quiet place and cook chips? Thankfully I had a couple of wonderfully trained managers from other stores assisting me in-store, and Paula Ryan from Darlington McDonalds worked on drive-thru all day—an absolute rock.

Franchisees were the worst; they were busy checking out the new equipment, chatting to my staff and getting free Cheeseburgers with the vouchers from the local paper. Some were jealous of the first McMaze playground in South Australia and spent ages looking it over. Other franchisees took turns standing out in the drive-thru lane criticising my Colorbond cladding over brick choice—very disruptive. One even had the gall to sit in the dining-room chatting up my full-time female manager.

The rest of the day passed in a blur. The sales for the day were only $1,802 and my overarching memory of the day is just wishing all non-paying people would leave.

Of course I'd overcommitted myself with full-time staff to ensure good service regardless of sales, which was part of my business plan to give outstanding service. Over the next month I focussed on my deep discounting commitment, as it takes at least a month to turn new customers into loyal ones. My marketing consultant advised me that no-one wins a price war, but I believed a meal deal discount paired with great service would drive people in, and keep them coming back. As the customer count goes up there's a chance they will become regulars and trade into full-price items.

The discount plan consisted of $2 breakfast, with a switch to $2 dinner cheeseburger meals after 5 pm and two Big Macs for $3 all day, every day. Some local franchisees were put out by my strategy and claimed I was doing harm to the brand particularly at breakfast, but I knew I had to drive sales growth quickly if I was to survive.

About three weeks after opening, once all the opening day creases were ironed out, the frantic nature of the new store eased and I had time to think. I sat in the back room, hair askew, unable to remember if I'd eaten that morning. Should I have stayed with Tony? He'd offered a house of my choice in Melbourne if I continued working with him. I could have accepted a training position at McDonald's Melbourne head office. But I had signed a lease for a house and all my worldly possessions were in rapid transit towards my new home.

On cue, as though she'd read my thoughts, Bronwyn the Regional Training Manager for Victoria, Tasmania, South Australia and Western Australia arrived from Melbourne. Knowing she was a close friend, a crew member showed her through to my office.

'Mich, why don't I run the store for a couple of days while you have a rest? That'll also give me a chance to brush up on the new equipment ready for the managers' class here next week.'

Grateful and exhausted beyond measure, I gladly accepted her offer and handed over the keys and the rosters. I retreated to my new home and concentrated on unpacking the boxes that had finally arrived from Melbourne.

While I was gone, Bronwyn calibrated every piece of equipment in the store. She hounded technicians to repair, replace and resolve problems. She ran mini-service meetings and preventative maintenance classes for managers and key full-time crew. She assisted in fine-tuning the ordering and roster systems, all while motivating and uplifting the exhausted crew with tales of Melbourne sales volumes. She also filled them in on my path to this new role as the tenth franchisee—and first female—in South Australia.

Chapter 17

Now Hiring

The second-most frequently asked question I get asked, after 'how much money does a McDonald's store cost?' is 'what's the best way for my child to get a job at McDonald's?' Here are some common sense basics:

1. Call the store where you want to work and ask for the correct spelling of the hiring manager's name.
2. Hand deliver or post your résumé, personally addressed to the hiring manager—old fashioned but effective.
3. Follow up a few days later with a phone call or visit.

I am aware of the McDonald's new online employment site but if you work by the principals above you can be in front of a very long online queue. Once you have an interview:

1. Be punctual and do not, I repeat, do not chew gum. If they hire you, you'll soon understand the aversion to gum; as a crew member you will have to scrape off every filthy piece stuck under thirty plus tables and benches before the Full Field.
2. There's nothing wrong with wearing school uniform unless you are in your 30s. Neat casual is fine.

3. Have a list of questions to show you have given the process some thought.
4. Don't be afraid to ask the pay rate.
5. Leave your 50-metre swim certificate at home.

School reports were a useful tool in the interview process; as an exercise I once asked my managers to bring in an old report. Each mirrored their current traits. God bless teachers; they know us better than anyone. My year twelve report read 'must learn to apply herself in class' and 'must stop distracting others.'

Part of the interviewing process in the 1980s was to challenge interviewees to add up several menu items on a menu order pad without the aid of a calculator or register. Registers then didn't have buttons for individual items so maths skills were essential. Then the total of the order was keyed in and change given without the aid of the register flashing the amount of change due.

As a manager, it's important to get a clear picture of someone's strengths and weaknesses at the interview. When reading school reports, I paid particular attention to attitude, school absences and recorded sick days.

Next I would engage the applicant in normal conversation and once they'd relaxed a little, the information flow could be enlightening.

'I notice you were absent from school a few days last term.'

'Yeah, I took a few Fridays off to go to the snow.'

'Great. Does the whole family ski?'

'Yeah. We have an apartment at Mount Buller and ski every weekend.'

'What do you do as a family over the Christmas break?'

'We go to our beach house.'

Next applicant please.

When applicants are 15 or 16 years old you're hiring the parents as well. Parents usually manage their children's rosters, organise transport to and from work, and wash and iron the uniform. Many years ago I minded my godchild overnight. He worked at my store and while he stayed with me I considered it was my duty to iron his uniform. He won a Best Appearance pin that day.

With this in mind I decided to revamp the parent/crew nights at the Cheltenham store in 1988, which I held regularly for new and existing employees. The previous set-up saw parents sitting quietly in a hall being encouraged to ask questions while their children sat next to them like in a school assembly. Young employees often chose not to invite their parents, viewing the whole thing as uncool and embarrassing—like a mass parent/teacher evening. But I wanted families to see first-hand why the crew had to be on time, the dexterity that was required of them and the sheer physical and mental toil expected of them by their managers, team members and customers.

I contacted parents and invited them—and any siblings—to work alongside their kids in the store on regular Monday evenings. The acceptance rate was almost one hundred per cent. Four crew and up to two members of their family were rostered on the areas of front counter, drive-thru and unloading of the delivery truck. I often placed dads in the dining room to reverse gender roles a bit.

On arrival, crew and family members donned name tags then watched an introductory video in the crew room downstairs, before the kids got a chance to shine and show off.

It was great to see a child proudly instructing his mother on the correct way to dress a Big Mac, while the mum struggled to get the burger neatly into the old-style foam container. Another child laughed as her mother tried to make a 30 cent Soft Serve Cone, losing more Soft Serve to the counter than the cone. It was priceless hearing a child instruct his father how to mop the dining room floor without walking back over it, with the man's neighbours looking on from a nearby table. A father charged with unloading a truck told me, as he rubbed his hands together in the freezer, that he had never worked so hard in his life.

After the rush we'd grab a free meal and sit together in that sparkling clean dining room. My initiative brought plenty of rewards: crew who were habitually late started to arrive on time, general presentation improved and there were fewer last-minute sickies. There was greater understanding from parents if managers needed to replace shifts or if staff finished late on a busy night. We built a stronger bond within the whole team and it was one of the innovations I was most proud of during my McDonald's career.

Later in 1991 I was involved in the first ever Parent Opinion Survey, which I thought was an important addition to the annual National Crew Opinion Survey. Results from that first survey showed that 96% of parents of our employees aged under 18 thought that McDonalds provided a good work experience for their teenagers.

Back to the hiring process. As the interview progressed, further investigative powers were needed.

'Have you spoken to your parents about working at McDonald's?'

'They said it was OK.'
'How will you get to work?'
'They'll drive me.'

Often parents had no idea about the shifts agreed to, or that they could clash with sport or school commitments, nor about the transportation duties that were being assigned to them. Kids made promises with the intention of just getting the job and then dealing with practicalities later.

The next stage of the interview dealt with an applicant's availability and here we emphasised that honesty was the best policy.

I asked one girl how often she could work.

'Thursdays between 3.30 pm and 4.30 pm, and Sundays between 2 pm and 4 pm.'

'Right. That's not very often, really. What else do you to?'

'Well, I go out Friday and Saturday nights and I have ballet training during the week.'

Maybe she was a little too honest? Still, we went through each week day and negotiated her working alternate Fridays and Saturdays, to allow for the all important social life and ballet.

I know a lot of people think we only hired very young people. Each store has its own policies, but I always found a mix of school and university students, part-time and full-time employees to be the backbone of a successful store.

Along with cash registers that provide all the answers, technology advances meant I no longer had a reason to speak with and catch-up with parents. Sadly the use of mobile phones and texts in later years prevented me talking to parents directly.

Often entire families will work at McDonald's and a

parental cheer goes up when the last child graduates from the store—no more smelly shoes or late night pick-ups. I have chatted to many parents waiting in McDonald's car parks to collect their children. Thankfully in Adelaide, kids get their driving license at 16.

The main goal in hiring is to employ reliable people who will stick around for a long time. You hope that they enjoy their job, feel safe, make friends and go on to other jobs with portable skills. Once you hire a staff member they often maintain a long-term connection to you throughout their life, whether looking for personal references for jobs or house leases or even inviting you to their wedding. I took hiring personally and still feel enormous satisfaction on hearing what my past employees have achieved.

I liked to hire paper deliverers because that is a tough gig; also guides and scouts because of their outgoing personalities and team awareness. Another hint: I used to ask the potential hire's friends at the store if they would employ them. They were usually honest and answered the question seriously.

So now you have the job. If not, try again in a few months time, as you may be asked for a second interview. We all dislike interviews, but practise is important. Practise with someone who will take you through your paces. Remember in 1982 Don Kissell gave me a shot and it worked.

Chapter 18

Would You Like a Smile with That?

The cop-like knock on my office door at the Fulham Gardens store in April 1993 meant trouble. We'd only been in business for four months.

'Mich, a customer just chucked their Big Mac at Sarah!'

Pushing back my stool, I marched to the front counter. To get upset and formally complain about service or food was one thing, but to hurl food and assault my staff was a different matter. The customer was unlikely to be right today.

'Get Sarah off front counter now,' I muttered under my breath as I stepped up to face the customer. The other front counter crew members had already moved back from the counter, as per their training for conflict situations.

The short, wiry, dishevelled woman peppered her swear-word diatribe with just enough information for me to gather she didn't like the taste of her burger. 'I want to speak to a real manager,' she yelled finally. 'I want my money back and I want that girl fired!'

While you might think the front counter exists to present

food, hold cash registers and Ronald McDonald House money-boxes, and for small children to sit on, at times like this it became a moat; a barrier between Us and Them, and a place of refuge while I considered my options. I stood quietly for a few seconds, remembering the first rule of dealing with customer complaints—just listen.

When she drew breath, I firmly asked her to 'Leave now.'

She threw her medium fries at me to which I responded, 'You're banned from this store forever.'

'Bitch. I'm gonna call Head Office.'

Ah, the Head Office threat. Why did people use it? It certainly never made me tremble.

From out the back Dave yelled, 'I've called the cops.'

Undeterred, the customer came to my favourite part—the attempt to gain support from onlookers in the store. 'Don't eat at this dump!' she yelled as she turned towards the crowd. 'It's a rip off. I'm going to sue!'

When you hear a tirade of abuse unleashed on an undeserving party, it's human nature to side with the underdog. Sarah was popular with customers and crew; several customers spoke up quickly to defend her.

'Get a life, Bitch. It's just a burger.'

'How would you like someone to throw food at you?'

'She's just doing her job.'

Pretending to be getting on with the business of serving, I kept one eye on the woman while awaiting the police. I heard a whoosh of air and ducked just in time as a dining-room chair flew past my head and clattered against the drink station.

'We'll take it from here.' A collective sigh could be heard as two policemen escorted the woman outside.

She pushed and shoved, yelling 'That bitch can't ban me from the store. I'm a paying customer!' Her voice was drowned out as she was helped into the back of the police car.

All this fuss and it was only 10.42 am.

Other complaints were less physical.

'McDonald's Cheltenham. Can I help you?'

'I got takeaway at your store and there was no sauce for my nuggets. It happens all the time and I'm sick of it.'

'May I have your name please?' I always asked this first, so I could politely use their name throughout the call.

'No you can't. But I want yours, so when I ring Head Office they'll know who to sort out.'

I sighed. *The Head Office threat again.* 'But I just ...'

'Now, listen to me ... Where is the customer service?'

Another deep sigh. 'We don't sell nuggets. Perhaps you went to Red Rooster over the road?'

Silence followed by a dead phone line.

'McDonald's Rundle Mall East, can I help you?'

'Last night my husband bought a Happy Meal for our son but we didn't get a toy.'

'I'm very sorry about that.'

'How dumb are your staff that they can't even get that right?'

'May I have your name and address so I can post a voucher for you to use on your next visit?'

'Don't bother. I need to go back to Myers after work, so I'll pick it up then.'

'You've actually called the Rundle Mall East store, not the Myer Centre, but if you come here I would be glad to replace your Happy Meal, including the toy.'

Clunk. Conversation over.

Some complaints bordered on the bizarre and required a creative solution. In the thick of a lunchtime rush at the Fulham store one gentleman refused to move his car out of the drive-thru lane until we exchanged his Happy Meal toy for one he didn't already have. He turned his car engine off, folded his arms and sat staring straight ahead, ignoring car horns and pleading staff. The toy he wanted was from Hungry Jack's but no amount of explaining would convince him of that. It wasn't until a complete set of four shiny new toys in their plastic bags were handed over that he cheered up, started his engine and moved off. I muttered a bemused, 'Hope to see you again soon,' as he departed.

When I was a struggling university student, one way to save money was to go to any Macca's and tell them a fictitious story about missing or cold burgers, and they would hand over free food. There was even a website dedicated to excuses a hungry person could use. In response to this scam, the system was eventually changed and vouchers were posted to home addresses, thereby creating a record of claimants.

But the best type of customer complaint was one that actually helped the business. A manager with an open approach could learn a lot from these interactions. Once a Cheltenham customer complained that the men's toilets were often dirty first thing in the morning, but that he wasn't surprised. On questioning him further, he suggested it might be because I'd reduced the cleaner's hours.

'Actually I haven't,' I frowned.

'But I see him leaving the store at 2 am every morning on my way home from work,' he said.

Hiding in my new silver Honda, part of my store manager's package, I witnessed a 2 am departure and a 5 am return, just prior to the breakfast manager's arrival, all while he was clocked on. That particular cleaner's hours were significantly reduced forthwith.

Another time a casual conversation with Muzz, a former store manager at Fulham and past employee from Cheltenham, revealed that on some Friday nights the outside lights and signs were turned off at 9.30 pm.

'Why have you started closing so early on a Friday night?' he asked me.

We weren't, but it transpired that one of the managers regularly turned them off in order to appear shut. He figured it was a great way to clean up and get home early.

Other managers could get distracted from the core business of selling food. Once, after spending an hour trying to call the store from home, I had to fax a duty manager a hastily scrawled message, 'GET OFF THE PHONE!'

But my all-time favourite example of constructive feedback went to Tony Cataudo, a McDonald's supplier in South Australia. He sat in my Fulham Gardens store drive-thru one night for 18 minutes and was still eight cars away from ordering. Eventually he got out of his car, walked inside the store, into the manager's office, and told his daughter to get off the phone and do her job.

Complaints came in as many forms as those full-field sheets: missing product, slow service, staff behaviour, cold product, soda water instead of lemonade and messy dining rooms. More serious offences were short-changing customers, food poisoning and slips and falls.

The only case of food poisoning on my watch was handled by the local council, as it's always preferable to have an external authority investigate. Even if customers came back to the store with a complaint, we'd advise the council as compliance with health regulations is one of their mandated responsibilities. When the council employee turned up unannounced to do his investigation, we were happy to oblige. His final report vindicated us completely. A Filet-O-Fish had been purchased in the morning, left on the back seat of a car for a couple of hours on a hot day, and later fed to a hungry six-year-old child for lunch. I was able to avoid a costly outcome for Macca's that day.

At Cheltenham one day a workman from the council wanted to discuss closing off the side road for road works. When I came to talk to him he looked me up and down before insisting, 'I want to speak to the big boss.' By which he meant, 'I want to speak to a man.' At that time there were very few female managers, and I guess some men had trouble with that. Coming from a family that believed a good education and hard work were all you needed to succeed, I found the lack of respect due to my gender annoying. Fortunately most of the men I worked with over the years treated me with respect. On that occasion I fetched the franchisee, Uncle Tony (as we affectionately called him) who stated in a deep man-voice, 'Michele IS the boss,' before walking away.

And yes, often complaints stem from genuine concerns. I too have gone through a drive-thru only to leave without syrup for my hotcakes, napkins (my pet hate) and with Coke instead of Diet Coke. Why don't we check our orders before we drive off? And while I'm on a roll, would it hurt stores to clean the drive-thru windows and surrounding area? They're all I get to look at while waiting and they are often filthy.

Although customer complaints and issues are the most obvious items to resolve, with 80 to 120 mostly teenaged staff in my care, parental liaison formed a large and rewarding part of my role. And you thought only customers had issues.

One young girl's mother made an appointment to discuss her daughter's rosters. We sat at a small corner table in the dining room with a coffee and made polite conversation until she brought up what was troubling her.

'Mich, why has my daughter been rostered for the close shift (8 pm–2 am) every Friday and Saturday night recently?'

'She shouldn't be,' I said. 'Let me grab last month's rosters.'

On inspection there was no sign of her name on any late-night shifts, or on swapped shifts or sick leave replacement. The mother frowned, stood up, thanked me and left.

Overall I felt there were some boundaries as to how much should be discussed with an employee's parent.

'Why has Adam been suspended?' An angry parent phoned in to ask.

'What did he tell you?'

'Nothing, as usual.'

'I'm sorry, but he needs to speak to you himself.'

Within half-an-hour Adam and his dad were at the front counter.

'May we speak to you privately, please?'

When we entered my office Adam blurted out, 'I'm sorry for swearing at you.'

His dad explained, 'I did not bring up my son to have a foul mouth. We're sorry for any trouble and it won't happen again, I assure you.'

As I watched the father push his son out the office door, I believed him. And I felt for Adam.

When another father demanded to know why his daughter was suspended I refused to tell him. He then informed me he was a reporter for the local press, and that he would drag my name through the mud. Under duress I told him about the inappropriate behaviour that had occurred between his daughter and a male crew person downstairs in the staff room. He apologised for threatening me, and we never spoke of the matter again. His daughter went on to be very successful in life.

Sometimes my strict rules of conduct were undermined. Once I fired a girl for giving away free food.

'But it was only a 30 cent cone,' complained her mother.

Following her formal complaint, the union insisted I reinstate her. The poor girl had worked extra hours apparently and claimed she did not know what she was doing, though her smirk when I reinstated her belied this.

I always tried to treat enquiries from parents with respect and a genuine desire to resolve issues, but a few interactions with parents really put me to the test.

'How old are you, Michele?' asked another disgruntled parent after I'd spoken to his son about always arriving late for work.

'At my age I don't have to answer that.'

'What would you know? You don't have children.'

While that was true, it had seemed sensible to me that the problem could be resolved if the teenager rode his bike to work, rather than wait for his perpetually late father to drive him. I guess the father thought another parent would have more compassion.

Then there were the crew members who simply didn't show up at all. Or parents who phoned in the middle of the Saturday lunch-rush to say things like, 'little Johnny won't be in today because it's Grandma's birthday.' Amidst the ensuing short-staffed chaos, the franchisee or head office consultant might drop in and express concern at the slow service, dirty dining room or toilets, or the backed up drive-thru. It would've been nice to be able to explain it all away—staff shortage, new trainees, three bus-loads of lost tourists—but invariably there was no time for, nor interest in, explanations. The expectation was that we would masterfully repair anything which was amiss. Magic wand anyone?

Fortunately most parents were thankful for and supportive of their children's work opportunity, and from some parental complaints came longstanding innovations. My favourite example was a father who was concerned about his son collecting rubbish in the car park and surrounding neighbourhood. David Willsmore wasn't worried about the actual activity, but the method. He arrived at my store one day with two sets of long-handled barbeque tongs and gardening gloves. A year later—after I'd told Head Office about it—a long-handled pick-up-tool became standard issue in all stores to prevent needle-stick injury. I wish we had designed and patented that idea.

And then there was the mother who was comfortable about her daughter collecting rubbish and performing parking lot pickups, but wanted another crew member or manager to accompany her for safety after dark. Absolutely.

An illuminating conversation I once had with a mum came about when I attempted to transfer her son to another store. He was dating a female manager and it was not an ideal situation. When asked why he and not his girlfriend was being transferred I candidly replied that a manger would be harder to replace. She kindly pointed out to me that that was not fair. It was still discrimination and she helped me to see that.

A father complained after I lost my cool one day and told his son he 'wasn't fit to take the garbage out'. I gave the son a genuine public apology and learned another one of those on-the-job lessons: never discipline in anger. I continued to be taught new lessons by customers, parents and crew until the day I left McDonald's. Of course it wasn't only customers and parents of staff who complained. The backbone of any business—the staff—also had their say.

A popular method of internal staff communication was the Crew and Manager Rap Sessions. Held quarterly, they lasted about an hour and gave everyone an opportunity to air grievances and promote new ideas. Minutes were taken and a week later, after many discussions and much thought, solutions were displayed on the notice board. These meetings often circumvented problem situations before they festered into formal complaints from the staff. I learnt that it was vital not to dwell on certain topics or become too negative.

Manager rap sessions were conducted by a store manager from another store. From our State Co-op meetings I developed friendships with other franchisees, and we would exchange trusted store managers to perform this important task. The crew rap sessions were usually conducted by my Store Manager, who chose a cross section of crew from different days and shifts to gather and represent their peers' ideas and concerns to management.

Funnily enough the main topics were food related: a need for microwave ovens to warm up meals from home, increase staff meal allowances for full and part-timers, and enhancing the staff meal allowance to include casuals. Once staff ID cards commenced, which allowed McDonald's employees to buy discounted meals at any store, there was a noticeable decrease in theft of food.

Topics that never seemed to disappear from the minutes were: managers not helping on shift, managers being too busy (or bludging) in the office and not helping out on the floor, and a request for more staff get-togethers which baffled me. I figured we were together during my 60-70 hour working weeks. Time alone please.

A lack of respect received by newly promoted staff was another regular grievance. A new manager called Ricardo once pointed to his name badge and declared, 'I am the manager' to fits of laughter and mimicry from his colleagues. What he had yet to learn is that respect is earned—it doesn't come automatically with the name badge.

Then there was the classic, 'I've been here longer than her. Why did she get promoted before me?'

'Let me think ... she always turns up on time, and is precise, professional and courteous. Next?'

At one crew review I questioned a young employee about regularly not appearing in full uniform on her set Friday night shift. Because it was always flat out when she arrived, I'd lend her bits and pieces out of the uniform cupboard. At her crew review the chance arose to discuss the matter.

'Mich, may I have a second uniform please?'

'But you only work once a week. Surely that's enough time to wash and iron it?'

She stared at the floor. 'Mum and Dad have just separated and I need one at each house. I'm at different houses every weekend and it's hard to keep track of things.'

Why hadn't I thought of that? It was so easy to be busy with rules and the black-and-white of life. Note to self: remember the grey. 'Let's get one for you now.'

I once had a young man beg me for five months to train him on front counter. This was at a rather sexist time in our history when the boys worked out the back cooking the food, and the girls worked at the front counter. At his crew review he explained his two mates out the back were driving him crazy. He wanted to work hard and become a manager. When I relented, he quickly learnt the ropes and went on to become an outstanding manager and won many awards. At the other end of the scale, my crew informed me a well-regarded manager was allowing them to pay him petrol money if he kindly drove them home after work.

As a Franchisee I had the opportunity to state my point of view at the biennial Franchisee Review, attended by the Regional Manager, my consultant and I. My number one item for the two-way feedback session was always about my desire to own a second store. Other topics involved staff training and promotions, and my thoughts on Head Office staff improvements. In turn I was always praised on my sales increases, commitment to staff training, and my willingness to help other franchisees.

There was also an annual written survey McDonald's

conducted with all franchisees. The survey was fun because it was anonymous. Employee relations rang me once after I tried to skew the results by ticking that I was a male with three stores in Tasmania. How did they know it was me?

I didn't need to wait for annual surveys or biennial reviews, as I always felt I could pick up the phone anytime to speak with the CEO or department heads. I was comfortable calling Head Office and never hesitated to ask questions or make constructive suggestions about sponsorships or product rollouts.

My feedback varied. Once I complained about the semi-regular cancellation of managers' courses in South Australia when attendee quotas weren't met. Head Office suggested we send managers interstate instead, but that meant accommodation, flights and food costs were payable by the franchisee, making it too expensive. I felt it unfair my staff had to miss out because other franchisees hadn't taken up the opportunity, and wanted Head Office to run the courses regardless of numbers. They did take this on later when my friend and Regional Training Manager Bronwyn supported my suggestion.

Later on, when I was President of the South Australian Co-operative, I asked management to address the fact that there was no fridge or storage facilities for after-work beverages in the South Australian Head Office on Greenhill Road. The South Australian state manager, later a Sydney franchisee, sorted that situation.

Another area that I felt needed improvement was communication within the stores. We needed a solution to the mass of untidy notes on the notice board and signs everywhere announcing new procedures, suggestions, ideas and general staff news. I created and edited the McChelt Chatter, a monthly newsletter combining essential staff communiqués along with a healthy dose of humour. The idea was adopted years later by Head Office to communicate with all stores in the state, which they called The Sauce.

Generally complaints made by manager's were about the lack of respect from those above them in the food chain, the long hours and the lack of recognition by superiors for a job well done.

While complaints were unfortunately common, it was always rewarding to receive compliments and thanks over the years. I received letters when staff got the (post-McDonald's) job they'd wanted, bought a new car or succeeded at exams I'd helped them get time off for.

I remember one kid called Jarrod who, on hearing I'd sold my first store and was leaving McDonald's, asked, 'Mich, you're not leaving because of me, are you?'

'No Jarrod. You've always been a challenge but you are not the reason.'

There was an appreciative mum who sent me a Christmas card for years. Her son had had learning difficulties at school but through a school-based training program worked at my Fulham Gardens store every Friday for two years. He loved it, starred in the training courses and we were thrilled to have him. Reliable, neat and polite; he was the perfect crew member. This young man eventually got an apprenticeship and became a carpenter, though I would have happily kept him on.

Chapter 19

Many Happy Returns

On Friday nights the phone rang constantly with birthday party bookings and queries. Callers would confirm party numbers, attempt (usually in vain) to make last minute bookings, or try to change existing party timeslots.

To avoid this onerous task I'd buzz the intercom downstairs and inform the unfortunate office manager at the other end that it was for them. Within a couple of minutes the patsy would appear, roll her eyes at me, open the manager's cupboard and take out the brightly covered day-to-an-opening Birthday Diary before responding to the caller.

'What date would you like?'

Parties were organised with military precision. A year in advance the party diary was ruled up, with set times displayed at two-hourly intervals: one-and-a-half hours for each party, thirty minutes to clean and prepare for the next onslaught. The Cheltenham train carriage that managers often wished had been destroyed in the fire, was divided into sections. Depending on numbers, up to four parties could be held at staggered fifteen-minute intervals. Often the last party didn't leave the station until 7.30 pm.

Some days would be ruled as NO BOOKINGS: McHappy

Day because it was the busiest day of the year; Mother's Day as it was the busiest breakfast in the year; and public holidays, because wages were expensive. Arguments would always ensue: 'But it's Hannah-Eve Lynne's birthday that day.'

The whole process was taken seriously and we were all held to account for transgressions. The devil was in the detail and that was certainly the case when dealing with party procedures. At a Managers' meeting, Sarah, the Community Relations Representative (CRR) and 'queen' of party planning stared us down.

'Who booked a party out of the prescribed times on Saturday and, worse, used a pen?'

It might seem petty but there were reasons for the strict adherence to protocols. When numbers were updated frequently and bookings moved or cancelled, the details could be amended easily when pencilled in. Mind you, good luck trying to find a sharpened pencil let alone a rubber at any McDonald's shared desk; there was usually a nice piece of frayed string hanging empty in the party diary. So on this occasion I confessed.

'It was me. The customer was screaming at me about movie times and in a weak moment I gave in.' Never again did I change the set times, or use anything other than a pencil.

Part of Sarah's job was to order and pack the party goodie bags prior to each weekend. Each party pack was filled with a small gift: either a plastic straw, a spinning top (or to save money, an old Happy Meal toy), a balloon that in those days you blew up yourself, (today they're filled with helium, another expense), and a free French Fries or small soft drink voucher to encourage a return visit. A party hat was placed in front of each child's tray mat, with party packs handed out by the hostess and a specially-wrapped birthday present given to the guest of honour.

Sarah as the CRR was the only employee with a key to the party storage cupboard. If party numbers changed or people turned up uninvited and items were short, staff rang Sarah at home. She would come to work and fix the situation even on her days off. Some parents would stop at nothing. You'd think with McDonald's being so procedurally fixated there'd be a policy to cover situations like that, but there wasn't, and franchisees watched every dollar in the 1980s—even the few coins it took to cut another key. Of course the expensive items in the Party Cupboard would have been a factor; Ronald watches and dolls, Grimace towels and slippers, free Big Mac vouchers, raffle prizes, gifts for school fetes, sporting encouragement awards and $5 complaint-appeasement vouchers were all easily stolen, so only highly trusted staff were given access.

'Can we book Ronald? We'll pay for him.'

'That will be $1500 ...' While the world-famous clown wasn't actually available to entertain party-goers, we found this approach more effective, and grinned at their shocked reply.

'What?'

Or, 'My child has been invited to Josh's party at your store tomorrow, but we've lost the invitation. Can you tell me what time it starts?'

Definitely not. We could not release that private information. There were occasions where non-custodial parents involved in divorce disputes were keen to see a child on his or her birthday. They'd attempt to extract information from the staff but our policy was to apologise, explain and suggest leaving a return phone number so we could pass it on to the party parent.

The best ruse I heard was, 'There will be three children and thirty adults, but the adults won't be eating. They'll just have a coffee. How much will that cost?'

Did I explain that coffee was free for adults at children's parties? Until the arrival of McCafe and Espresso Pronto coffee in 1993, thirty coffees required five brewed pots, at seven minutes per pot. With only one machine that meant our regular customers would have time to join the dots on a Ronald tray mat and read the daily newspaper before getting their morning brew. Not ideal.

Eventually minimum booking numbers were introduced. Six children at $2.95 would at least cover the food cost. 'But I only have three children to bring, not six.' Confusion still reigned.

Hosting birthday parties cost stores money but were very important to the business of children. Why? Because McDonald's sceptics might be converted. How do parents tell a child, 'You can't go to Josh's party because McDonald's isn't good for you?' Or tell them they can't go to a land where they can have soft drinks, a burger and fries, play games, run around with their mates, and finish off with an ice-cream cake. McDonald's children's parties were a good cheap option. No cleaning the house beforehand or after, invitations and birthday cake supplied and no prying parents hanging around your house.

Dealing with mix-ups might go like this:

'Hi I'm Murray, your party Hostess.'

'I thought you had an Aquarium-theme party room?'

'No, we don't.'

'I was told over the phone you did. Get me the manager.'

'How can I help?'

'One of your staff has stuffed up my party booking.'

On cue a husband might comment, 'Hang on. Didn't we book at McDonald's Camden?'

Staff were inevitably stretched when parties turned up without a booking, on the wrong day or at the wrong store. With tensions and expectations running high as guests arrived, tables would be quickly cleared in the dining room, paper tray mats would be flipped over to do double duty and, God willing, a sharp pencil would be on hand to scribble 'Party' on the back (blank pieces of paper were very hard to come by in the days before computers and printers were installed in every store). A front-counter crew member would be dispatched to introduce themselves as the hostess and the CRR would be contacted to open the treasure cupboard.

It took a special type of crew person to be trained as a party hostess. High level organisational skills, patience and imagination were mandatory. They also needed an ability to juggle balls and people, the strength of character to discipline ten-year-old boys and lots of energy. An artist's touch could also be handy for those rainy days. A grown-up fairy princess ruling her kingdom was the ideal candidate.

My first experience of a McDonald's party as a customer was at an impromptu 21st at Camberwell. There was no playground so we wheeled the birthday girl, crowned with a cardboard party hat, in a plastic high chair down Burke Road. We were fuelled not by alcohol, but by litres of bright orange

Fanta. Camberwell Macca's doesn't exist anymore. We could have told them back in 1979 that they needed a playground.

For the stores without playgrounds a favourite party activity for children aged eight years and up was a tour behind-the-scenes. The party hostess would take them inside the freezer, turn off the lights and wait for the squeals of delight. We also gave store tours to Brownies, Cubs and school groups and the freezer was a popular destination. Imagine if that happened now? Games were 'musical chairs' followed by 'pass the parcel' with more old Happy Meal toys and free food vouchers for all guests in between each layer of newspaper, and a packet/box of cookies as the main prize for the birthday child. The finale was 'pin the tail on Ronald'.

In the late 1980s around Australia there was a recall of wooden playgrounds after it was found that some treated wood contained arsenic. Thankfully I never witnessed a child chewing the ladders to reach the top of the outpost on the wooden fort at Cheltenham. But overnight the playground disappeared and our imaginations had to come into play to entertain party children.

And who was the bright spark who invented the whirly roundabouts? You know the ones that spin and spin, round and round. Even writing about it makes me giddy. Our roundabout had Grimace, the purple blimp, in the middle as decoration. He was aptly named: a twisted expression, expressing pain, disgust or wry amusement. Kids would alight from the roundabout and throw up in the tanbark daily and it was me who grimaced the most while cleaning it up—being in management was so 'high brow'.

At the Fulham Gardens store I later owned, a playground

with slides was installed with ladders and a helicopter on the very top, state of the art and made of plastic. Often a customer would need our help:

'Can you get Barry/Lucinda/Casey out? They're stuck.'

Well into my late thirties by then, I struggled to climb into the high tunnels—not a good look. It was no wonder many female managers swapped skirts for trousers as part of their uniform.

Plastic balls in playgrounds were another potential hazard. Not a choking hazard; little kids would pee on them and then the playground had to be shut down while the balls were washed and sanitised. I'd like to know how Ikea manages.

Because of the party train, our Cheltenham store was booked out months in advance. At various times we held state and national records for the most parties held weekly, monthly and annually. In later years, my own franchise at Fulham broke many a party record.

In the 1990s, separate party rooms with interactive activities were built inside or next to the stores—finally, the munchkins had their own zone. More importantly, other customers could finally dine in peace without the need for earplugs; no longer were they caught in the middle of a fries crossfire, or forced to watch fizzed-up party kids see how far they could spit soft drink through dozens of straws joined together. Perhaps that's why drive-thru was invented?

When I was offered a promotion from Cheltenham store manager to Fulham Gardens franchisee in 1992 I could see the yet-to-be-built store's potential. I had a large wall-mounted snakes-and-ladders game and crazy mirrors installed, to help grow the party numbers. The kids giggled at their own warped bodies but roared with laughter at the adults' shapes. Toddlers, with their mouths and mitts covered in Ketchup would gleefully smear the immaculate mirrors and kiss their reflection. The 1995 addition of a purpose-built party room meant we could comfortably host 32 children at a time.

Some families supplied their own cake: spectacular, intricate Barbie mansions; football jumpers in team colours; or Ninja Turtles. The cake often had to rest precariously atop frequently needed items in the kitchen fridge and a shift manager's greatest fear was the possibility of damage prior to the singing of 'Happy Birthday'.

First thing Saturday morning the manager would add up party numbers and check our cake supply, as most families were happy with the Macca's version. If there weren't enough cakes for the day's bookings, a crew member would bolt to the nearest supermarket and purchase all the Peter's ice-cream cakes. The firm rule was one cake per ten paying guests.

I remember when I was still managing the Cheltenham store, there was uproar from my senior manager because he saw two cakes for a party of ten on my shift.

'Don't you listen? They should only have one cake.'

'Let me explain ...'

'You will have to charge them extra.'

'Already have. They're twins.'

Often a dining-room customer would see the delicious ice-cream cake with candles making its way to the party room and want one, right then and there, for their own birthday child.

'I'll get someone onto it.'

But which someone? There were no spare crew. Somehow we'd have to manage—the customer is always right. The $5.00

cost included the cake, candles, plates, spoons and a crew member to cut it up and sing Happy Birthday. We couldn't just leave them to it, as knives were not allowed to roam the dining room unattended. So party knives—and the cake slicers which eventually replaced them—hung out with party-booking pencils and matches (smokers would take them) in the locked party cupboard, because otherwise you could never find them when needed. The only McDonald's item I didn't run out of in 26 years was party plates. They came in boxes of 2,500.

Thirty years on, parties can be booked online. There is a God.

Chapter 20

Flag Protocol

It amazes me the lack of knowledge some Australians have about how to treat our flag. Flag protocol is taught at Girl Guides and Scouts but it wasn't part of the school curriculum. During my twenty-six years at McDonald's, I'd watched staff allow the flag to touch the ground when raising or lowering it, place the flag upside down or even position the McDonald's flag above the Australian National Flag. All of these sins contravene the Australian National Flag Protocol. When eagle-eyed customers, usually returned service men and women, noticed these slips complaints came thick and fast.

When purchasing my Fulham Gardens store in Adelaide in 1992, I ordered dual flagpoles to alleviate at least one of those potential issues but another soon presented itself. Which pole does the Australian Flag go on? According to military protocol, the Australian National Flag should be flown on the left when facing the flagpoles, just as soldiers wear their medals on the left breast, while family members may wear their ancestors medals, but only on the right breast. I tried putting an Australian Flag sticker on the pole to the left while facing the building (heart side) but even that wasn't foolproof. Teaching the crew to always raise the Australian Flag first and lower it last, and to ensure it always flew freely and as close as possible to the top of the flagpole with the rope tightly secured, took more time than you could imagine.

The flag would often be left up after dusk which is another no-no unless it's properly illuminated. If I arrived at the store at 8 am and no flag was displayed it was a sure sign the maintenance man hadn't arrived, as it was his job to raise the flag every morning. Once the breakfast menu was added the flag raising time became 5 am or first light, whichever came first.

In the McDonald's 'Orientation Video' for new staff you'll see Aaron, one of my crew members, demonstrating how to raise the Australian Flag the correct way at my Fulham store. He had been taught first-hand by a customer I'd approached to give my staff a lesson on flag protocol. Watching old Reginald, a World War II veteran, teach Aaron how to fold the flag with dignity and respect brought tears to my eyes.

Even raising the Australian Flag to half-mast has its own protocol. The flag must be raised quickly to the top of the pole and then lowered 'ceremoniously' to half-mast (which is slightly above halfway). An acceptable position would be when the top of the flag is a third of the distance down from the top of the flagpole. On Australia Day, Anzac Day and Remembrance Day, I was even more diligent about checking the flags. On sombre occasions such as these, the McDonald's flag would not be flown at all. Head Office eventually implemented email reminders to stores on the relevant days and fewer mistakes occurred.

There was just one protocol I personally had trouble with. The rule to never fly the flag if it is damaged, faded or dilapidated meant that we were supposed to destroy the flag 'privately and in a dignified way such as by cutting it into small unrecognisable pieces before disposing in the normal rubbish collection'. This I could never do. Thus I have a number of old dilapidated Australian flags at home, along with my collection of McDonald's and Olympic flags.

All of these concerns became redundant when the last store I owned, Rundle Mall East in Adelaide City, didn't have a flagpole at all.

Chapter 21

Crew Uniforms

The first Macca's uniforms were large blue smocks worn over people's own clothes, with a light-blue paper hat. But there were some issues with the paper hats. While cleaning the glass behind the fry station heating elements, a crew member's hat would occasionally catch alight. Windy days were also a problem, as hats would be blown off during travel paths and rubbish pickups. They were also easily snatched from your head to the taunts of teenage customers whilst you swept and mopped the dining room. And managers got cross if more than one was required per shift, as over time it caused a major dent to profits.

Next came the new polyester one-size-fits-all elasticised unisex pants and top that didn't need to be ironed. The new uniforms came in yellow, brown and blue. By sticking to one colour for all the staff, it was easier for the manager to order more when new crew were hired. Everyone looked the same, just like a school uniform. It may come as no surprise, but no one liked yellow, as it looked terrible against most people's complexion. Managers tended not to like having everyone in brown as it blurred the lines between crew and managers. So the blue uniforms became the most popular colour.

A fault with an elasticised waist, the pants were easily pulled down by prankster crew members.

To address these issues the subsequent uniform design included a stiffened fabric visor, a tie or bowtie to wear with a fitted shirt, name badge and grey pants with belt loops and a belt. Six items instead of three. Only one visor was issued per staff member. I am told the visor is a sought-after fashion item when McDonald's introduced baseball caps.

When the paper crew hat was replaced with the visor, the old paper hats became an iconic item within the McDonald's world. They were spray-painted silver and presented to managers at training classes as a contested award. The Silver Hat was presented on the last day of class by a head office representative or a franchisee. It was a coveted award because it was voted on by peers, and awarded to the manager who 'conducted and represented themselves in an admirable and outstanding fashion', framed and signed by your class members. After I became a franchisee several of my managers received The Silver Hat. But I never won one during my time as a manager.

Staff were responsible for laundering their own uniforms, and if you worked more than three shifts per week, you were issued with a second set.

While not a frequent event, new uniforms did seem to come around more often than strictly necessary. First we had the blue smocks, then the one-size fits-all, striped shirts and visors, then black shirts with yellow stripes, then grey, red and black shirts (designed by a crew member through an internal competition). This was followed by my favourite uniform—black polo fitted shirts, belt, buckle and baseball cap all designed by Peter Morrissey, and combined with crew-supplied pants just after I left in 2009. And now we have the red shirts with greyish jean lookalike pants.

As a franchisee I was usually hesitant to replace 100 uniforms at around $50 a piece. Crew were required to pay a deposit when receiving their uniform, which was refunded to them when they resigned and returned their uniform. If the uniforms were in reasonable condition franchisees would reissue them to an incoming new crew member after being washed. Yuk. Thankfully this recycling practise has ceased. Once or twice I was able to sell unused sets of the out-dated uniforms to another franchisee who wasn't updating to the new style straight away.

Like the party cupboard, the uniform cupboard was scrutinised as closely as sales takings, bank debt and expensive equipment. Uniform stocks were counted monthly as part of the End of Month Stat, and usually only the store manager and training manager had a key to the cupboard. If a crew member accidentally left something at home, they'd beg, borrow or steal a replacement, hence the locked cupboard, as it was another cost to the franchisee. Some crew would leave their uniforms at the store in unlocked lockers when they knocked off, scrunched up in a ball.

The designer and the company who supplied the new uniforms in 2000 did their homework on the quality, durability and most importantly they designed them to be easy to wash. Later on when crew had to iron fitted shirts and keep track of the many extra items included in the uniform, items were often left at home. With the introduction of aprons for both front and back crew it was another thing to keep track of. And we'd thought losing name badges was an issue.

Uniforms were tricky to stock without any idea as to the sizing of potential crew. After my early experience of being stuck wearing the men's uniform, I made sure I kept one size of each, especially for new female employees to try on during orientation, as some girls wanted a baggy fit, and others liked to wear them skin tight. But too often stores would end up with unused stock, as once an item had been opened and tried on, the supplier wouldn't take it back. As Head Office wasn't involved, the best you could do was swap or sell them to another store. It may sound ridiculous, but keeping on top of uniforms was one of the hardest internal systems to manage.

Chapter 22

Co-operatively Speaking

At my first South Australian McDonald's Co-Operative Quarterly Marketing Meeting I wore my manager's uniform because I had been working at the store from 2 am finishing off the February 1993 month-end count, pays and monthly bookwork. I tried to be on time but was held up running orders to cars in the drive-thru parking bays, answering the phone and marking off last-minute deliveries. Why did the Marketing Department schedule a meeting on the first day of the month, when they ought to have known it's always administratively chaotic because of end-of-month processes? Obviously someone who wasn't in close contact with their franchisees.

It was suits and ties all round except for myself and two other new franchisees wearing managers' uniform—there was no handbook for this stuff. I had secretly wanted to make an excuse and stay at the store. I'd already met all the franchisees over the previous few weeks but the idea of being in a room with all of them as well as Sydney Head Office representatives made me feel hot and uncomfortable. My nerves were bound to show through.

Each state had it's own Co-Operative, belonging to all the

franchisees in the state, so that common issues and concerns could be discussed, and processes for implementing company policy could be agreed. Each year a president and treasurer were elected by the members to manage budgets, expenditure and marketing plans.

A curious thing was the agenda starting time. Perhaps one day I will understand what '8 am for an 8.30 start' actually means.

Order was called, coffees grabbed and into the meeting room we went. I chose to sit with the men wearing managers' uniforms for some camaraderie, in our dress sense at least. Introductions were made around the table. I really wanted a cigarette. Sitting quietly with eyes down, I waited until it was my turn to speak. I then asked about equipment, product and suppliers. At morning coffee the state manager took me aside and explained the Co-Op meeting was not about 'my store issues' but about marketing. Where was that in the franchisee handbook?

'Your consultant can help you iron out those details.'

Great. Now it was confirmed. I was an idiot.

When I re-entered the meeting room for round two the mood had shifted.

I was looking the other way when someone sat on my lap.

'Are they treating you properly?' It was our new Australian CEO Charlie Bell. 'I thought I'd check you've settled in to your new home.'

I gave a nervous laugh. He remained perched on my lap for what felt like forever, not-so-subtly emphasizing our closeness as all eyes were on us.

How was I doing? It was a good question. Firstly, I'd

been reported by a franchisee for sitting in a gutter smoking with a manager and had to attend an appointment with state management to discuss my behaviour. This was during the construction phase and there'd been nowhere to sit so we'd perched on the lip of the drive-thru curb to have a chat. Then a different franchisee had told me in strict confidence that the other South Australian franchisees regarded me as a company store manager who would do their bidding. Oh, and my closest neighbour had banned his staff from food transfers to my store because he had applied to buy the Fulham Gardens franchise and had his nose out of joint. (When opening a new store it is helpful to borrow product from your nearest neighbour until sales and ordering have settled into a reliable a pattern.)

'It's been quite a ride,' I finally responded.

'Good, good,' he nodded, and departed as quietly as he'd arrived.

As our discussions were confidential we fell silent whenever hotel staff entered the room. We treated them as if they were spies from our main competitor, Hungry Jack's.

As the owner of a new store, I was incredibly time-poor, and resented the imposition of this day-long meeting. I could hardly afford to take a cigarette or lunch break (yes, I took up smoking again due to stress), let alone an entire day away from running shifts, running Monday's payroll, ordering supplies and paying bills. The upside of these meetings was that they gave me a chance to converse with adults rather than my mostly teenaged staff, and learn about the other business activities, banking, finance, profit/loss, leases and how to deal with local councils and the McDonald's hierarchy.

At the conclusion of that first day-long meeting I felt a

sense of relief that it was over, but also glad I had turned up and gained a better understanding of this aspect of the business. A sneaky goal entered the back of my mind as I reflected on my initially cool reception; I'm going to run this one day.

The quarterly meetings could turn into shouting matches and name calling at times. At one fiery meeting, when I was still the only woman in the room, I was asked to leave so that I wouldn't hear the swearing. Another time chairs were shoved around and a franchisee stormed out leaving his stunned wife behind. Much later, when I was president and demanded quiet during a particularly vocal and emotional meeting about the Ronald McDonald House charities, one of the elder statesmen asked, 'Have you got PMT?'

Hiding my shock at his insolence I replied, 'Although it's none of your concern, I am pre, post and present and I demand this conversation be minuted!' I knew for a fact that Charlie Bell read the minutes of every state marketing meeting, and wanted him to know about this outrageously sexist question.

South Australian franchisees were passionate about AFL, kids' soccer, meal-deal specials, and deep discounting such as the $2 dinner meals in order to win business from other fast-food chains, and we'd regularly argue over the percentage of sales contribution to the National Advertising and Marketing Fund. Although South Australia had the second lowest state sales, we were on a growth spurt with new franchisees coming into the system regularly, and we had a history of being strong and insisting on having a say on how the marketing dollars would be spent. Unlike other states with up to sixty franchisees attending Co-op meetings, with only eleven of us we could quickly unite, gather momentum and make decisions very quickly. We were the first state to trial many new initiatives, such as salads, The Big One burger to take on Hungry Jack's Whopper, Face-to-Face Drive-Thru, upsizing and meal deals. Hungry Jacks' sales were still higher than ours so we were always thinking of new ways to grow sales and increase profit. Our Co-op's main contribution to the system was 'Made for You' in 2003, a radical change from a production bin with only ready-to-eat product.

The annual Company Roadshow, which the Head Office marketing department ran every year to explain the promotions and marketing budgets to each state's franchisees, always started in South Australia and then moved clockwise around the country. At their next stop in Western Australia the marketing gurus would tell that state's franchisees that we had voted yes to most issues, almost daring them to refuse. This would continue around the country until they finished up back in Sydney.

In general we were quick to say yes to crew scholarships, but no—initially—to sponsoring netball. There was a resounding yes to the Eisteddfod sponsorship (another Charlie Bell initiative) but no to sponsoring the Adelaide Crows in 1993. This was just before the Port Adelaide Football Club joined the AFL in 1994. There was unanimous approval for sponsoring the South East Asian Rainforest at the Adelaide Zoo, but then we gave the junior tennis tournament away.

Requests for sponsorship dollars were received daily. It was hard to say no to clubs and groups desperate for money but budgets had to be maintained. For example, in our first full year Fulham Gardens' sales reached $1 million so I contributed $47,500 to the National Marketing Fund, in addition to my sponsorship of local businesses, schools or sporting clubs. Requests for basketball tops, orange bowls and courtesy cups, donations for raffles and school fundraising hopes came out of a category called promotions on my store Profit and Loss statement.

My local community got to know me and how to best request sponsorship. Most were weekly sports encouragement awards and annual trophies. I never presented an award or trophy personally, preferring to send another staff representative as I was shy. Some franchisees have been presenting awards for over 30 years.

Apart from the mandatory State Co-operative Committee, franchisees were expected to rotate through other committees or represent McDonald's on other boards, such as Tennis Australia, Auskick and state Eisteddfods. Some committees were permanent, while others evolved over time.

The South Australian Public Relations Committee was the umbrella group for managing our involvement in Tennis SA, Adelaide Zoo and Ronald McDonald House. In 1995 our Co-Op donated $180,000 to the Adelaide Zoo to help build a South East Asian Rainforest Exhibit. Crew scholarship winners were also decided by the Co-Op chair and state or marketing manager. Part of the judging was on an essay written by applicants. It was inspiring to read these and I introduced an interview process because I wanted to meet the people behind the written word. The study scholarships were worth $1500 and I always asked what they were planning to do with the money if they won—another initiative of the South Australian Co-Op.

South Australia was ahead of most states in sustainability,

having implemented a recycling system with cash refunds for bottles and cans in 1977. I signed up to the South Australian Government Litter Strategy Committee as the McDonald's representative and worked towards ending the use of plastic shopping bags, implementing fines for cigarette butts in the street and funding for an independent group KESAB. The Keep South Australia Beautiful organisation was the first litter-reduction campaign in the county when it formed in 1966. Some individuals in Adelaide had their own ideas about litter. One man, obviously not fond of our product, was known to collect McDonald's rubbish from around the city, store it in his garage and then send photos to local newspapers. He sometimes dumped full garbage bags in various store car parks.

At the end of my first Co-Op year I stood for election onto the Co-Op Executive Committee. The Executive Committee comprised five franchisees chosen from the eleven members of the Co-op. From these five, one would be voted chair. I was voted in—which wasn't difficult with only five standing for election. But what experience did I have? My marketing background consisted only of delivering the advertised product as best I could, but Head Office had whispered in my ear that it would be good for my career.

The following year I stood for Co-Op President in the mistaken belief that doing so increased my chances of getting a second and third store. A week before the election I contacted six franchisees to gather votes. One said no due to my lack of experience, saying the hours I needed to spend in my store as a new franchisee would not allow me enough time to devote to the position. Another said that because I was Victorian I didn't understand South Australian issues.

As the votes were being tallied I felt a wave of nausea. Why had I put my hand up for this? The outgoing president had rallied behind me and promised me support from the Co-Op. A prerequisite was to be a member of the Executive Committee and I was easily re-elected. Once the Executive was formed, the other four elected members would then vote for the president of the Co-op. In the end, three of the four elected members supported me, one abstained, and no-one stood against me.

Flushed with pride and red cheeks, I moved to the end of the boardroom table, thanked everyone for their confidence and wished the outgoing president hearty thanks. Now to run the meeting. The South Australian Marketing Manager was my crutch that day and I followed the prepared agenda carefully. I felt such relief when I announced 'morning break' and got a cheer.

The McDonald's corporate staff congratulated me and as I posed for the obligatory public relations shots, I was glad I'd worn my new navy-blue David Jones suit and matching high heels, with a fresh haircut. An article appeared in the 20th December 1996 edition of the Adelaide Advertiser newspaper the following day announcing my election but unfortunately there was no accompanying image. I was rather disappointed given I had just become the first female president of a state co-operative in McDonald's history.

Chapter 23

Is This A Paid Position?

I found myself starting work at Fulham Gardens earlier in the mornings to get my store work completed before my daily Co-Op President duties kicked in. I was determined to perform well at both to prove the doubters wrong. My Dad kept asking, 'Why are you doing it when you're already so short of time?' To which I always answered, 'This is how I get another store.'

Throughout 1996 and 1997, at least twice a week, I met with the state marketing manager and we spoke on the phone every day. We'd check that budgets and marketing promotions were on track, that is, ensure that the marketing spend was having the desired effect on the state's overall sales. I learnt to be conservative with sales projections because the four per cent of total South Australian gross sales, which made up our marketing spend, was based on that prediction and I did not want the South Australian Co-Op in debt. If the actual sales were less than projected, and we'd spent the four per cent of projected sales, that meant the following year the Co-Op would start off in deficit. The Corporation paid for our advertising and marketing up front, and then the Co-Op would pay them back at the end of each year. The McDonald's state manager projected sales for new stores and was always way above actual figures. Posting a deficit also meant cutting back on TV advertising or planned programs or saying no to sponsorship requests.

Maintaining a healthy relationship between the Co-Op and the Corporation was vital because the alternative meant each franchisee had to put their hand in their own pocket to negate the debt, and as I've learnt, it's extremely difficult to separate a franchisee from their money.

In my first franchise year, the South Australian state manager commuted every week from Victoria and often needed convincing about South Australia's uniqueness. For instance Santa arrives on Pageant Day and travels down the Adelaide Mall to his Magic Cave in the David Jones store. This has been happening on the second Saturday of November every year since 1933, and draws huge crowds of families to watch the hundreds of floats, sets and entertainers. In order to benefit from this unique heritage event, franchisees requested that the McDonald's Christmas calendars be delivered to Adelaide stores prior to that weekend, which is well ahead of the normal Australia-wide distribution. Unique also to South Australia was the fact that iced coffee outsold 600ml Coca-Cola bottles and so we requested it be added as a menu item. And Hungry Jack's was the preferred fast food restaurant even though 'the burgers were not better at Hungry Jack's'.

Our most successful promotion was the annual mailer with it's glossy pictures and deep discounts spread over the quiet time called February.

I served as Co-Op President for two consecutive years, and filled in the following year when the new chair had a health scare. As President I was invited to many functions: the cricket as a guest of Channel 9, Olympic dinners, football dinners and Tennis Australia events. I met many famous athletes who were all so generous with their time and eager to support grassroots sport for children.

As a group of franchisees we sometimes scheduled secret meetings, without inviting McDonald's company personnel. Strangely the Company always knew where and when these meetings were being held and who had said what during each meeting. I guess like any group of humans, we had our moles. On one occasion as Co-Op President I suggested we should invite a company representative to attend. I then figured the gentleman who protested the loudest was most definitely a traitor/the mole. We were our own worst enemies, and so competitive about gaining multi-store ownership, our antics were sometimes similar to schoolyard behaviour. There were a couple of leaders of different groups, followers, bullies, the kid no-one talked to, the new kid on the block, the dobber, the teacher's pet and of course the rebel. I'd flourished at school, so this environment was not new to me.

Once as president, I decided to book a meeting room at a café, away from our usual venues. I thought it would be less formal, easier to discuss matters out of earshot of the corporation and was hoping for better food and beverage service than the typical convention centre. We were upstairs and the noise from downstairs diners made it difficult to hear. The café's lunch rush was in full swing and our designated waitress had been pulled away to wait on outside tables. The meeting at this venue turned into a nightmare. Eventually one franchisee, who habitually undermined me, stood up and addressed the group.

'This is ridiculous. We should all move to my office in the city.'

Frustrated and embarrassed, I left the meeting and marched up the street towards my home about 800 metres away. I was angry with myself, and all too aware of my error in trying to do something different. I didn't need others to point it out. Suddenly I heard someone approach.

'Mich. Come back. We've booked the pub over the road. There's a room upstairs.'

Two franchisees had quietly dealt with the situation in a professional manner. Thankfully the tears did not come. I composed myself and marched back. From that day forth if I booked a new venue I visited it as a guest first. I would sit on my own in a room that caters for 60, and tasting everything on the menu that I wanted to serve to the Co-Op. I was never caught out like that again.

When I was finally offered the chance to buy another store it was on the same day I had made an appointment with our state manager to inform her I had decided to sell up and move back to Melbourne. I had joined every committee, assisted new franchisees and given my entire life to the business. After 26 years I'd decided to say farewell. I was tired, ready to return to my family in Melbourne and needing to leave on a high. The voting and Co-Ops were no longer enjoyable and I continued to lose motions. My last vote was a well-fought battle to get something I valued over the line.

A wonderful external speaker had for an hour and a half vigorously presented and discussed the importance of our menu and the perceived relationship with obesity. He told us obesity was the next smoking / lung cancer dilemma. Several companies had full-time departments dedicated to resolving obesity issues and we needed to listen up and get on board. He thanked us for listening. Half an hour later, after the sales projections and budget slide presentation, we voted on financial support for Little Athletics State Wide. Nabbie the marketing manager was passionate about the sponsorship and had worked hard with the Little Athletics organisation to nail a reasonable sponsorship package that would be beneficial to all.

Seven voted for and nine against. There was uproar. Had the naysayers not paid any attention to the previous speaker? With the support of two other franchisees I demanded we vote again. A good friend used his proxy from an absentee franchisee and I said I had another franchisee's proxy. Our Co-Op rules state that a proxy must be in writing which I usually had but on this occasion only verbal. No one checked or challenged my proxy. The vote went ahead again: eight yes and eight no. People started yelling and pointing fingers and some even walked out of the meeting, at which I shook my head in disbelief. We implored the company representative to exercise his rarely used vote and break the tie. The Co-Op President (not me this time, unfortunately) could cast a deciding vote to break a dead-lock. Both didn't exercise their power to vote, and so the motion didn't carry.

The next day page three of *The Adelaide Advertiser* announced 'McDonald's pulls the plug on Little Aths'. Later that week everyone saw sense and finally accepted the state-wide sponsorship deal.

But it was too late for me—that week in 2007 McDonald's first female state manager accepted her only female franchisee's decision to leave the system.

Chapter 24

Be Daring, First and Different

Monthly sales increases were the sole aim of the business, and we had lots of ways to entice customers to visit us more often. Promotional burgers, limited-time-only shakes (do you remember shakes the flavour and colour of the Olympic rings whenever the Games were on?) and the then infrequently offered Happy Meals with collectable toys drove increased transactions. When I started at Macca's, weekly Happy Meals were a thing of the future, once we'd worked out how to capitalise on the incredible power of children's nagging.

We were notified, encouraged and congratulated daily, weekly, monthly and quarterly. I often received congratulatory memos from State Head Office for having broken previous daily, weekly and monthly sales records. Some of them were hand-signed by Charlie Bell, then Field Service Manager in the 1980s.

Top ten sales and transaction count comparisons around Australia were collated and posted, and action plans for improvement were written by each store. When the new Cheltenham store reopened after the 22nd October 1984 fire, our sales went through the roof. Each week, each month, each quarter was a great improvement on the previous one.

The brand-new store, with more modern décor and a brighter dining room all helped, as did the leap in staff morale. Ultimately we came 9th in Australia in 1988 with a massive 19.67% sales increase on the previous year.

In 1987 there was a Shanghai McNugget promotion, to put some fun back into the system. Head Office offered financial incentives for the best decorated store, average cheque increase (meaning dollar spend per customer) and local store marketing (LSM) extensions, which involved fun ideas for marketing at the individual store level. At my stores we regularly had dress-up days where all the staff wore costumes, and we'd give prizes to local school kids who took on our theme. In this way we could support local schools in fundraising for new playgrounds or sports equipment, AND increase our takings at the same time.

Around the time of the 1996 Summer Olympics in Atlanta, a manager at my Fulham Gardens store had the store lawn painted with the Olympic rings and won a trip for two to America. Great for them but I had to pay for the artwork. Mind you, the lawn did look impressive.

Regular communication throughout the company was vital to promoting a sales focused culture. We received regular memos from Head Office called 'Hot off the Grill' and published our in-house newsletter the *McChelt Chatter* at Cheltenham, which included McDo's, McDont's, McOscars and McMichie's Predictions. There was a regular Australia-wide publication called 'Crews N Views' and the McAdelaide quarterly newsletter as well, all designed to motivate the staff to improve their service and profitability.

'Crew Member of the Month' and 'Crew Member of the Quarter' awards are still valued to this day. Crew would be rewarded with pins for their area of expertise, such as '60 Second Service', 'Secret Service', 'Best Grill Man' and 'Dangology'—awarded to the crew member who could have the customer's order bagged up and hanging out the drive-thru window before they got to the payment booth.

At Rundle Mall East I regularly ordered pins for Fast Hands, Employee of the Month, Star Performer, Safety Team, Clean Crew, Best Wrapped, Morning Crew, Night Crew, Grill Master, Fast & Friendly Service

Other awards we received were the 'Touch of Service Speedie', 'Look to your Future', 'Service with a Smile', 'Doin' the Wrap', and 'Taking Charge'. An electrician who did regular repair work for us once gave me a pin 'Recharge Your Kitchen' as a promotional gimmick, as he knew how much McDonald's crew loved their pins.

My favourite award was 'Be Daring, Be First and Different', which was given to managers for a good shift. While I hate to blow my own trumpet, I'm told I must include details of the awards my team and I won.

When I redeveloped my Fulham Gardens restaurant in October 1994 so that that customers received face-to-face service in drive-thru, little did I realise the impact it would have. I was the first franchisee in Australia to implement this. Prior to this customers in the drive-thru gave their order into a speaker box, much like they do now, but I decided to trial having a person take customer orders face-to-face at the first box before driving to the cashier and pickup windows. We built the new standalone box near the start of the drive-thru, installed wireless communications and updated the landscaping. Drivers perceived that the service was faster, and therefore they were more likely to come back and use it again. It didn't take long to see the sales growth, measured in dollar increase, cars served per hour and the increase in drive-thru sales as a percentage of overall take. Mine went up to over 50% of our total store take. My success was the precursor to all restaurants in South Australia adopting this system. In 1996 McDonald's Australia awarded my Fulham Gardens store the 'Outstanding Drive-Thru Award, recognising our superior operations and appropriate reinvestment; deliver an outstanding drive-thru experience to my customers'. However the fact-to-face system wasn't for everyone, and was eventually phased out. You can still see some box windows boarded up.

At my Fulham Gardens store I instigated the Birthday Club. Children who held a birthday party at our store were given a complimentary membership to our Birthday Club, which gave them discounts all year round as well as free food offers, gifts on their birthday, puzzles, and colouring-in competitions in the mail. It encouraged return customers, rewarded loyalty, and gave us some great demographic information. McDonald's later took this concept and turned it into the Ronald McDonald's Funland Club in South Australia, and at one point had a database of over 30,000 families.

My greatest contribution to McDonald's Group policy was initiating the South Australian Sales Building program in 1998, which evolved from concerns about inconsistent discounting practices across the state. Many franchisees felt we were working against each other rather than with each other. I developed the program to drive sales and maximize local store marketing while taking advantage of economies of scale by pooling our resources, and to encourage our state franchisees to work better together as a group.

In 2002 while owning Fulham Gardens, I won the Franchisee of the Year Award for South Australia. A non-McDonald's award by the Franchise Council of Australia, it recognised my efforts in sales leadership and training, public relations, contributions to group policy development and initiatives benefiting the local community. I felt honoured to be recognised for my efforts, which included eight years serving on the Executive Committee for the McDonald's South Australian Cooperative, three years as President, and overseeing the development the South Australian Co-op's Constitution. During the ten years I'd owned Fulham Gardens I had doubled my weekly sales and continually achieved 10% growth despite aggressive competition in my area, and was always in the top ten sales results for South Australia.

The most sought-after award for franchisees and managers was The Ronald Award for which there could only be one winner in the region. This award was presented to an individual who had made outstanding contribution, be it local, regional or national, to the development of McDonald's image in the areas of advertising, promotion or public relations. While I never won the Ronald Award, striving for it always helped me be the best leader I could be.

Chapter 25

Simply About Charlie

Passionate about the brand, the people and the product, McDonald's Australia CEO Charlie Bell would drive around the country visiting drive-thrus, just like Ray Kroc who would secretly time cars in the McDonald's drive-thru opposite his office in Oakbrook. I had a sign at my drive-thru window warning my crew that if anyone ordered two Junior Burgers, a Filet-O-Fish and a small orange juice, it would be our CEO. These products were core menu items but not as popular as Cheese Burgers, Big Macs and Chicken Nuggets, so he wanted to check we had them available within their time limit of 10 minutes. Standard procedure was to have one fresh Junior Burger and one Filet-O-Fish available at all times, which meant throwing out approximately six of each product each hour. And the orange juice? It was delivered to stores frozen in 250 ml individual plastic bottles, and it was important for quality control that they were thawed and stored to procedure, and not handed over still frozen, or worse, warm because the bar fridge was either not at the right temperature, crammed full or not switched on. One day Charlie did visit Fulham Gardens and my guys were so excited to meet him and we were ready. He came inside and shook everyone's hand and presented Drive-Thru pins. A coveted award for crew but to receive it personally from the CEO was special.

I first met Charlie in 1982 when he was in Head Office Melbourne and I had started work at the South Oakleigh store. Charlie had become Australia's youngest store manager in 1979 at the age of 19, and was clearly on an ambitious path. We were about the same age—in our early 20s—and I was the only woman doing management training, and the only manager who had not previously been a crew member. It was a big deal at the time and he went out of his way to make me feel welcome. We got on well from the beginning. I never knew he would be CEO one day.

Charlie's meteoric rise continued when he joined McDonald's Australia's board in 1989 aged only 29. He remained one of my closest friends and went on to do wonderful things personally and professionally. I spent time with him socially when we both worked in Melbourne; we shared a passion for musicals, theatre, educational opportunities for staff, and a cheeky sense of humour. He encouraged me to continue sponsoring local Eisteddfods and crew scholarships when I became a franchisee.

When I moved to Adelaide to open the Fulham Gardens store he rang to check my accommodation was what I needed and that the interstate move wasn't too stressful. A few years after that when Charlie moved to Sydney to become CEO of Australia, whenever I had training trips to Sydney, I'd always visit him. At McDonald's conference dinners and the Annual Marketing dinners with the State Executive Body and President, he would always motion for me to sit next to him.

From French Fries to a Franchise

We never discussed business at these times—we were just two friends catching up.

It's 1993 and four people dressed in suits stand on Adelaide's busiest thoroughfare, King William Road. Charlie wants to share with us his idea of a new style of café, to be called 'Simply About Coffee'. His idea is for separate businesses, not attached to a McDonald's store, but still owned and run by existing McDonald's franchisees. He suggests building one in Norwood, one in King William Road and a third in the Marion Shopping Centre. We three fresh-faced franchisees are keen to try something new and exciting. We were honoured and humbled by Charlie's trust, and eager to operate these new concept shops.

Charlie took the 'Simply About Coffee' concept to the McDonald's Board but it was knocked back, later his concept became McCafe's around the world.

Tragically he died aged 44 of colon cancer. At his funeral in Sydney a song from his favourite musical, *The Boy from Oz* was performed live by Todd McKenney, "Just before I Go". Charlie was a showman until the end and I like to believe he's proud that I have finally completed my Diploma in Professional Writing and Editing, something we often discussed. To this day I still miss his advice, but most of all I miss his sense of humour.

Chapter 26

Hooroo, Now I'm A Macaroo

I'm proud of the fact that I was the fourth female franchisee for McDonald's Australia and the first in South Australia. I was not an experienced cashed-up businesswoman making another investment, nor was I an Australian McDonald's Head Office ex-staffer or ex-crew member; I was the very first female franchisee to come through the management ranks.

Now I was heading home to Melbourne, back the way I came with the same two cats, albeit in a better car. I was also carrying a valued gift from my former Co-Op colleagues, which they'd presented to me at my farewell dinner—I planned to use the Canon digital video camcorder as part of my Professional Writing and Editing course en route to becoming a famous short-story film producer and winner of the prestigious Tropfest.

Why did I leave Macca's? I could see, hear and taste the changes coming back then, they terrified me.

1. McCafe: a great idea but it would have taken me ten years to make a profit.

2. Compulsory 24-hour trading: I do not believe every store needs to be open 24 hours a day. Having said

that, I do not know what I would do without my local Prahran Macca's.
3. Cameras behind the counter covering staff areas and stock rooms: I always trusted my employees, and if not I believed cameras were not the solution.

There have been some changes since I left that I do love: a round ten McNuggets instead of the original nine; gluten-free cakes; and payWave for the drive-thru. I often imagine my improved service times through drive-thru and front counter if payWave had been invented then.

I said goodbye to McDonald's with some sadness when I sold my franchise in 2008. Now I eat French Fries that have been cooked and served by someone else, possibly by a future franchisee or CEO of McDonald's. I'm now a Macaroo, which translates (will the lingo ever stop?) to a retired McDonald's Owner/Operator. I am so proud of my non-expiring discount card with my name printed on it, and all the years of hard work and innovation that it represents. With this card I receive 20% off McDonald's food orders up to a maximum order value of $20 as well as discounts for hotels, banking, travel, car hire, petrol and insurance.

After a stint at TAFE studying for a diploma in professional writing and editing, playwriting, novel and short story writing, I returned to Macca's on a three month Store Manager contract at a suburban Melbourne McDonald's store. In the five years since I sold my last South Australian franchise there had been quite a few changes. At first the extensive menu range took me by surprise. There were so many new burgers and product variations: Angus Beef, a Grand Angus, and even a Baby Angus.

From French Fries to a Franchise

I mentally drew a DO NOT ENTER sign around the McCafe section. I had not trained to be a Barista. 'Soy latte with a double shot of espresso and extra hot milk on the side?' Please! Just trying to locate the symbols and signs on the register was enough of a nightmare for me. So to avoid McCafe McDisasters I implemented a policy to have a permanent employee in the McCafe with their own register at all times, which turned out to be a very good move. Our store soon had the highest percentage increase in sale volume and customers for three months in a Victorian McCafe.

On my first 24-hour overnight shift since 1983, I was training a new trainee manager and was glad I was there to assist when punches, chairs and saliva were thrown around the dining room at 3 am. Police were called, apologies made and hearts sent racing for all the wrong reasons. No staff were harmed during the incident but the dining room was absolutely trashed.

Then the cameras to assure the safety of the franchisees profit. I disagree with cameras in the workplace unless they are installed to protect the staff from customer harm. But I was curious as to their importance. In this store the registers were often short, float not balanced and the stock count way out with usage and ordering. A store's profitability depends on these systems being accurate. So what was the camera's function?

The tiny manager's office was cluttered with a computer and a monitor displaying nine live images from around the store, 24/7. I could see and hear drive-thru headsets accidentally left on, orders coming through loud and clear.

Buzzers announcing a car approaching the drive-thru and another buzzer announced the commencement of their order.

Suppliers were contacted by email or text, as were absent employees. Gone were the days of calling the household and getting to the truth of many matters. 'But aren't they are at work?' 'No they're not here; that's why I'm calling.'

The most vital piece of equipment in the business had become the computer, which is true of many workplaces, but I hated it. It had become the focus and took up most of the tiny manager's office desk. Now, managers were expected to spend their shifts watching screens on their own out the back. There were screens to watch the drive-thru, with service times streamed live to Head Office, screens showing the front counter register screens, EFTPOS screens and TV monitors. What about my headaches from these screens? Back office; front office; head office; manager's office and finally owner's office.

The only 'office' I had back in the day was outside near the dumpster, sitting on a milk crate. All the important decisions happened in that office. Managers and crew were spoken to about behaviour and training issues out there, along with plans for the next shift. Cigarettes were consumed outside AND out of the public eye as it had became a frowned-upon habit.

I felt I had returned to a completely different workplace. Verbal interaction was much reduced as the crew relied more heavily on screens and automated systems than on each other. One day I asked a staff member, 'Why does everyone go to the toilet so often?' They were as surprised by my question as I was by their answer: 'Because they're using their mobile phones!' When I banned the phones I sealed my fate. Neither managers nor crew spoke to me, and I became invisible apart from unavoidable interactions. At the end of my three-month contract I declined the offer to renew the contract again. It was a short-lived and fraught return to a business I had loved for just over a quarter of a century. I knew then I had made the right decision in 2007 to become a Macaroo.

CHAPTER 27

The Car Park

Sitting in my car at the McDonald's Melbourne Airport store car park one day in August 2010, while waiting for former McDonald's CEO Charlie Bell's daughter's flight to land, I casually observed a world-wide phenomenon. McDonald's car parks—especially those near an airport, busy shopping strip or venue where parking is at a premium—play host to some very interesting human behaviour.

There are two types of people in this world: people who pretend to be customers, even going so far as to enter the store and browse without buying before returning to their car, and there are the people like me who will make a purchase in order to feel comfortable accessing a free half-hour of parking.

The toilets were not bad for a 24 hour airport store. I watched as a young guy carrying a backpack ran into the arms of the woman parked behind me. They embraced briefly before jumping into her car and speeding off. A middle-aged couple looked around sheepishly as they walked their dog to and fro near the drive-thru entrance, obviously waiting for someone.

A car pulled up and three people exited and walked towards another parked car. There was much kissing, hand-shaking and a babble of loud conversation before suitcases were transferred from one car boot to another. Job done and a farewell wave. Again, no purchase. What was it about the McDonald's car park? Imagine if I parked at a petrol station bowser for 45 minutes without making a purchase? Imagine if my dog needed a toilet stop and I fancied some sushi from across the road, so I parked at the servo, wandered around until Fido did his business (and I didn't pick it up), ate my sushi, and then took off? Cafés don't let customers use their loo, drink their free water and read a newspaper without purchasing something, do they?

When I was second assistant manager at Elsternwick, my store manager advised me to buy large stickers printed with propaganda about the possibility of being towed away. We would carefully stick them on windscreens if people parked for a lengthy period of time without buying food. The only result was the odd irate customer screaming over the front counter, or the sight of drivers with their heads poked out the driver's side window leaving quietly. It really wasn't worth the stress of policing the car park.

Why did estranged parents choose the McDonald's car park to hand over their children? Was it the best neutral place they could think of? The promise of a treat for the child to soften the trauma? Perhaps the busyness of the car park was thought to quell a public outburst. Even McDonald's franchisees have been known to perform this task in their own or others car parks on Friday nights.

Another use for our car park was as a place of recreation for teenagers. They'd sit in their cars at night—sometimes for hours—laughing, talking, throwing rubbish out the window or emptying their ashtrays on the asphalt. Sometimes they'd even eat our food! At night I'd instruct the staff not to clean up the mess until the offenders had left because they'd often think it was amusing to throw more rubbish out of their windows to be spiteful or to get a laugh from their friends. We'd wait in pairs and with precision stealth sweep the asphalt clean immediately after they'd left. We didn't want rubbish left lying around to encourage other customers to litter too. A manager once threw rubbish straight back into a customer's car. I backed up her story when a phone complaint came through head office.

Young male managers and crew were often seen checking their own car's safety in the car park, and off-duty staff were often found hanging around while waiting for friends. Perhaps the demise of drive-in cinemas prompted the need for a new teenage hangout. It was relatively safe but with minimal supervision; just me doing a walk-through during my 30 minute travel paths.

As my phone beeped I was bought back to the present. I hadn't seen Charlie Bell's daughter Alex for twenty years, but we'd kept in touch over the phone, especially since Charlie's death five years earlier. I couldn't wait to see her and talk about Charlie. She was coming to discuss Charlie's posthumous 50th birthday celebration slated for November 2010.

Acknowledgements

Thank you to my mentor Hazel Edwards and to my editors Kathie Fisher, Lyndel Kennedy and Adam Sharp without whose support, ideas and ability to correct my grammar, this book would not have been finished.

Special thanks, to Teresa Anile for requesting "more detail" and working through massive edits.

My Holmesglen Non-Fiction writing group who workshopped my chapters.

Above all I thank my wonderful teachers and classmates at Holmesglen TAFE, Chadstone where I completed my Diploma in Professional Writing and Editing.

Thanks to Deb Vanderwerp, Ray Mooney, Kristen Henry, Mike Slusher, Gary Smith, Goldie Alexander and especially Teresa Cannon who taught me computer skills.

Thank you to my Maccas mates.

Kerry Wright (an actual Hamburger University Professor). Bronwyn Covill, Gerrie Richardson and Mike Goodluck have been my encyclopaedias about McDonald's history. Ian McNab (Nabbie) contributed chapter titles. Bergs Goodluck read an early full edition and suggested ways to make the book accessible for a non-McDonald's person.

Finally gratitude to Jane Curtain and Sylvie Blair for their professional publishing advice.

www.ingramcontent.com/pod-product-compliance
Lightning Source LLC
Chambersburg PA
CBHW042132160426
43199CB00021B/2885